CRISES OF THE REPUBLIC

BOOKS BY HANNAH ARENDT

The Origins of Totalitarianism

Rahel Varnhagen: The Life of a Jewish Woman

The Human Condition

Between Past and Future

On Revolution

Eichmann in Jerusalem

Men in Dark Times

On Violence

Crises of the Republic

The Life of the Mind:
ONE/THINKING
TWO/WILLING

Lectures on Kant's Political Philosophy

HANNAH ARENDT AND KARL JASPERS

Correspondence 1926–1969

HANNAH ARENDT AND MARY MCCARTHY

Between Friends: The Correspondence of Hannah Arendt
and Mary McCarthy, 1949–1975

CRISES OF THE REPUBLIC

Lying in Politics

Civil Disobedience

On Violence

Thoughts on Politics and
Revolution

HANNAH ARENDT

HarperCollins*Publishers*
Boston   New York

Mariner
An Imprint of HarperCollins Publishers, registered in the United States of America and/or other jurisdictions.
www.marinerbooks.com

"Civil Disobedience" originally appeared, in somewhat different form, in the *New Yorker*. Versions of the other essays originally appeared in the *New York Review of Books*.

ISBN 0-15-623200-6 (Harvest/pbk.)
Library of Congress Catalog Card Number: 72-187703
Printed in the United States of America

23 24 25 26 27 LBC 6 5 4 3 2

For Mary McCarthy in Friendship

CONTENTS

Lying in Politics

Reflections on the Pentagon Papers

"The picture of the world's greatest superpower killing or seriously injuring a thousand non-combatants a week, while trying to pound a tiny backward nation into submission on an issue whose merits are hotly disputed, is not a pretty one."

—Robert S. McNamara

I

THE PENTAGON PAPERS—as the forty-seven-volume "History of U.S. Decision-Making Process on Vietnam Policy" (commissioned by Secretary of Defense Robert S. McNamara in June 1967 and completed a year and a half later) has become known ever since the New York *Times* published, in June 1971, this top-secret, richly documented record of the American role in Indochina from World War II to May 1968—tell different stories, teach different lessons to different readers. Some claim they have only now understood that Vietnam was the "logical" outcome of the Cold War or the anti-Communist ideology, others that this is a unique opportunity to learn about decision-making processes in government, but most readers have by now agreed that the basic issue raised by the papers is deception. At any rate, it is quite obvious that this issue was uppermost in the minds of those who compiled *The Pentagon Papers* for the New York *Times,* and it is at least probable that this was also an issue for the team of writers who prepared the forty-seven volumes of the original study.[1] The famous credibility gap, which has been with us

[1] In the words of Leslie H. Gelb, who was in charge of the team: "Uppermost, of course, is the crucial question of governmental credibility." See "Today's Lessons from the Pentagon Papers," in *Life,* September 17, 1971.

for six long years, has suddenly opened up into an abyss. The quicksand of lying statements of all sorts, deceptions as well as self-deceptions, is apt to engulf any reader who wishes to probe this material, which, unhappily, he must recognize as the infrastructure of nearly a decade of United States foreign and domestic policy.

Because of the extravagant lengths to which the commitment to nontruthfulness in politics went on at the highest level of government, and because of the concomitant extent to which lying was permitted to proliferate throughout the ranks of all governmental services, military and civilian—the phony body counts of the "search-and-destroy" missions, the doctored after-damage reports of the air force,[2] the "progress" reports to Washington from the field written by subordinates who knew that their performance would be evaluated by their own reports[3]—one is easily tempted to forget the background of past history, itself not exactly a story of immaculate virtue, against which this newest episode must be seen and judged.

Secrecy—what diplomatically is called "discretion," as well as the *arcana imperii,* the mysteries of government— and deception, the deliberate falsehood and the outright lie used as legitimate means to achieve political ends, have been with us since the beginning of recorded history. Truthfulness has never been counted among the political virtues, and lies have always been regarded as justifiable tools in political dealings. Whoever reflects on these mat-

[2] Ralph Stavins, Richard J. Barnet, and Marcus G. Raskin, *Washington Plans an Aggressive War,* New York, 1971, pp. 185–187.

[3] Daniel Ellsberg, "The Quagmire Myth and the Stalemate Machine," in *Public Policy,* Spring 1971, pp. 262–263. See also Leslie H. Gelb, "Vietnam: The System Worked," in *Foreign Policy,* Summer 1971, p. 153.

ters can only be surprised by how little attention has been paid, in our tradition of philosophical and political thought, to their significance, on the one hand for the nature of action and, on the other, for the nature of our ability to deny in thought and word whatever happens to be the case. This active, aggressive capability is clearly different from our passive susceptibility to falling prey to error, illusion, the distortions of memory, and to whatever else can be blamed on the failings of our sensual and mental apparatus.

A characteristic of human action is that it always begins something new, and this does not mean that it is ever permitted to start *ab ovo*, to create *ex nihilo*. In order to make room for one's own action, something that was there before must be removed or destroyed, and things as they were before are changed. Such change would be impossible if we could not mentally remove ourselves from where we physically are located and *imagine* that things might as well be different from what they actually are. In other words, the deliberate denial of factual truth—the ability to lie—and the capacity to change facts—the ability to act—are interconnected; they owe their existence to the same source: imagination. It is by no means a matter of course that we can *say*, "The sun shines," when it actually is raining (the consequence of certain brain injuries is the loss of this capacity) ; rather, it indicates that while we are well equipped for the world, sensually as well as mentally, we are not fitted or embedded into it as one of its inalienable parts. We are *free* to change the world and to start something new in it. Without the mental freedom to deny or affirm existence, to say "yes" or "no"—not just to statements or propositions in order to express agreement or disagreement, but to things as they are given, beyond agreement or disagreement, to our organs of perception and cognition—no action would be possible; and action is of course the very stuff politics are made of.[4]

Hence, when we talk about lying, and especially about lying among acting men, let us remember that the lie did not creep into politics by some accident of human sinfulness. Moral outrage, for this reason alone, is not likely to make it disappear. The deliberate falsehood deals with *contingent* facts; that is, with matters that carry no inherent truth within themselves, no necessity to be as they are. Factual truths are never compellingly true. The historian knows how vulnerable is the whole texture of facts in which we spend our daily life; it is always in danger of being perforated by single lies or torn to shreds by the organized lying of groups, nations, or classes, or denied and distorted, often carefully covered up by reams of falsehoods or simply allowed to fall into oblivion. Facts need testimony to be remembered and trustworthy witnesses to be established in order to find a secure dwelling place in the domain of human affairs. From this, it follows that no factual statement can ever be beyond doubt—as secure and shielded against attack as, for instance, the statement that two and two make four.

It is this fragility that makes deception so very easy *up to a point,* and so tempting. It never comes into a conflict with reason, because things could indeed have been as the liar maintains they were. Lies are often much more plausible, more appealing to reason, than reality, since the liar has the great advantage of knowing beforehand what the audience wishes or expects to hear. He has prepared his story for public consumption with a careful eye to making it

[4] For more general considerations of the relation between truth and politics see my "Truth and Politics" in *Between Past and Future,* Second Edition, New York, 1968.

6

credible, whereas reality has the disconcerting habit of confronting us with the unexpected, for which we were not prepared.

Under normal circumstances the liar is defeated by reality, for which there is no substitute; no matter how large the tissue of falsehood that an experienced liar has to offer, it will never be large enough, even if he enlists the help of computers, to cover the immensity of factuality. The liar, who may get away with any number of single falsehoods, will find it impossible to get away with lying on principle. This is one of the lessons that could be learned from the totalitarian experiments and the totalitarian rulers' frightening confidence in the power of lying—in their ability, for instance, to rewrite history again and again to adapt the past to the "political line" of the present moment or to eliminate data that did not fit their ideology. Thus, in a socialist economy, they would deny that unemployment existed, the unemployed person simply becoming a non-person.

The results of such experiments when undertaken by those in possession of the means of violence are terrible enough, but lasting deception is not among them. There always comes the point beyond which lying becomes counterproductive. This point is reached when the audience to which the lies are addressed is forced to disregard altogether the distinguishing line between truth and falsehood in order to be able to survive. Truth or falsehood—it does not matter which any more, if your life depends on your acting as though you trusted; truth that can be relied on disappears entirely from public life, and with it the chief stabilizing factor in the ever-changing affairs of men.

To the many genres in the art of lying developed in the past, we must now add two more recent varieties. There is, *first*, the apparently innocuous one of the public-relations managers in government who learned their trade from the inventiveness of Madison Avenue. Public relations is but a variety of advertising; hence it has its origin in the consumer society, with its inordinate appetite for goods to be distributed through a market economy. The trouble with the mentality of the public-relations man is that he deals only in opinions and "good will," the readiness to buy, that is, in intangibles whose concrete reality is at a minimum. This means that for his inventions it may indeed look as though the sky is the limit, for he lacks the politician's power to act, to "create" facts, and, thus, that simple everyday reality that sets limits to power and brings the forces of imagination down to earth.

The only limitation to what the public-relations man does comes when he discovers that the same people who perhaps can be "manipulated" to buy a certain kind of soap cannot be manipulated—though, of course, they can be forced by terror—to "buy" opinions and political views. Therefore the psychological premise of human manipulability has become one of the chief wares that are sold on the market of common and learned opinion. But such doctrines do not change the way people form opinions or prevent them from acting according to their own lights. The only method short of terror to have real influence on their conduct is still the old carrot-and-stick approach. It is not surprising that the recent generation of intellectuals, who grew up in the insane atmosphere of rampant advertising and were taught that half of politics is "image-making" and the other half the art of making people believe in the imagery, should almost automatically fall back on the older adages of carrot and stick whenever the situation becomes too serious for "theory." To them, the greatest disappointment in the Vietnam adventure should have been the discovery that there are people with whom carrot-and-stick methods do not work either.

(Oddly enough, the only person likely to be an ideal victim of complete manipulation is the President of the United States. Because of the immensity of his job, he must surround himself with advisers, the "National Security Managers," as they have recently been called by Richard J. Barnet, who "exercise their power chiefly by filtering the information that reaches the President and by interpreting the outside world for him."[5] The President, one is tempted to argue, allegedly the most powerful man of the most powerful country, is the only person in this country whose range of choices can be predetermined. This, of course, can happen only if the executive branch has cut itself off from contact with the legislative powers of Congress; it is the logical outcome in our system of government when the Senate is being deprived of, or is reluctant to exercise, its powers to participate and advise in the conduct of foreign affairs. One of the Senate's functions, as we now know, is to shield the decision-making process against the transient moods and trends of society at large—in this case, the antics of our consumer society and the public-relations managers who cater to it.)

The *second* new variety of the art of lying, though less frequently met with in everyday life, plays a more important role in the Pentagon papers. It also appeals to much better men, to those, for example, who are likely to be found in the higher ranks of the civilian services. They are, in Neil Sheehan's felicitous phrase, professional "problem-solvers,"[6] and they were drawn into government from the universities and the various think tanks, some of them

[5] In Stavins, Barnet, Raskin, *op. cit.*, p. 199.

[6] *The Pentagon Papers,* as published by The New York Times. New York, 1971, p. xiv. My essay was prepared before the appearance of the editions published by the Government Printing Office and Beacon Press, and therefore is based only on the Bantam edition.

equipped with game theories and systems analyses, thus prepared, as they thought, to solve all the "problems" of foreign policy. A significant number of the authors of the McNamara study belong to this group, which consisted of eighteen military officers and eighteen civilians from think tanks, universities, and government services. They certainly "were not a flock of doves"—a mere "handful were critical of the U.S. commitment" in Vietnam[7]—and yet it is to them that we owe this truthful, though of course not complete, story of what happened inside the machinery of government.

The problem-solvers have been characterized as men of great self-confidence, who "seem rarely to doubt their ability to prevail," and they worked together with the members of the military of whom "the history remarks that they were 'men accustomed to winning.' "[8] We should not forget that we owe it to the problem-solvers' effort at impartial self-examination, rare among such people, that the actors' attempts at hiding their role behind a screen of self-protective secrecy (at least until they have completed their memoirs—in our century the most deceitful genre of literature) were frustrated. The basic integrity of those who wrote the report is beyond doubt; they could indeed be trusted by Secretary McNamara to produce an "encyclopedic and objective" report and "to let the chips fall where they may."[9]

But these moral qualities, which deserve admiration, clearly did not prevent them from participating for many years in the game of deceptions and falsehoods. Con-

[7] Leslie H. Gelb, *op. cit.* in *Life.*

[8] *The Pentagon Papers,* p. xiv.

[9] Leslie H. Gelb, in *Life.*

fident "of place, of education and accomplishment,"[10] they lied perhaps out of a mistaken patriotism. But the point is that they lied not so much for their country—certainly not for their country's survival, which was never at stake—as for its "image." In spite of their undoubted intelligence—it is manifest in many memos from their pens —they also believed that politics is but a variety of public relations, and they were taken in by all the bizarre psychological premises underlying this belief.

Still, they obviously were different from the ordinary image-makers. Their distinction lies in that they were problem-solvers as well. Hence they were not just intelligent, but prided themselves on being "rational," and they were indeed to a rather frightening degree above "sentimentality" and in love with "theory," the world of sheer mental effort. They were eager to find formulas, preferably expressed in a pseudo-mathematical language, that would unify the most disparate phenomena with which reality presented them; that is, they were eager to discover *laws* by which to explain and predict political and historical facts as though they were as necessary, and thus as reliable, as the physicists once believed natural phenomena to be.

However, unlike the natural scientist, who deals with matters that, whatever their origin, are not man-made or man-enacted, and that therefore can be observed, understood, and eventually even changed only through the most meticulous loyalty to factual, given reality, the historian, as well as the politician, deals with human affairs that owe their existence to man's capacity for action, and that means to man's relative freedom from things as they are. Men who act, to the extent that they feel themselves to be the masters of their own futures, will forever be tempted

10 *The Pentagon Papers,* p. xiv.

to make themselves masters of the past, too. Insofar as they have the appetite for action and are also in love with theories, they will hardly have the natural scientist's patience to wait until theories and hypothetical explanations are verified or denied by facts. Instead, they will be tempted to fit their reality—which, after all, was man-made to begin with and thus could have been otherwise—into their theory, thereby mentally getting rid of its disconcerting *contingency*.

Reason's aversion to contingency is very strong; it was Hegel, the father of grandiose history schemes, who held that "philosophical contemplation has no other intention than to eliminate the accidental."[11] Indeed, much of the modern arsenal of political theory—the game theories and systems analyses, the scenarios written for imagined "audiences," and the careful enumeration of, usually, three "options"—A, B, C—whereby A and C represent the opposite extremes and B the "logical" middle-of-the-road "solution" of the problem—has its source in this deep-seated aversion. The fallacy of such thinking begins with forcing the choices into mutually exclusive dilemmas; reality never presents us with anything so neat as premises for logical conclusions. The kind of thinking that presents both A and C as undesirable, therefore settles on B, hardly serves any other purpose than to divert the mind and blunt the judgment for the multitude of real possibilities. What these problem-solvers have in common with down-to-earth liars is the attempt to get rid of facts and the confidence that this should be possible because of the inherent contingency of facts.

11 *Die Philosophische Weltgeschichte. Entwurf von 1830:* "*Die philosophische Betrachtung hat keine andere Absicht als das Zufällige zu entfernen.*"

The truth of the matter is that this can never be done by either theory or opinion manipulation—as though a fact is safely removed from the world if only enough people believe in its nonexistence. It can be done only through radical destruction—as in the case of the murderer who *says* that Mrs. Smith has died and then goes and kills her. In the political domain, such destruction would have to be wholesale. Needless to say, there never existed on any level of government such a will to wholesale destruction, in spite of the fearful number of war crimes committed in the course of the Vietnam war. But even where this will is present, as it was in the case of both Hitler and Stalin, the power to achieve it would have to amount to omnipotence. In order to eliminate Trotsky's role from the history of the Russian Revolution, it is not enough to kill him and eliminate his name from all Russian records so long as one cannot kill all his contemporaries and wield power over the libraries and archives of all countries of the earth.

II

THAT CONCEALMENT, falsehood, and the role of the deliberate lie became the chief issues of the Pentagon papers, rather than illusion, error, miscalculation, and the like, is mainly due to the strange fact that the mistaken decisions and lying statements consistently violated the astoundingly accurate factual reports of the intelligence community, at least as recorded in the Bantam edition. The crucial point here is not merely that the policy of lying was hardly ever aimed at the enemy (this is one of the reasons why the papers do not reveal any military secrets that could fall under the Espionage Act), but was destined chiefly, if not exclusively, for domestic consumption, for propaganda at home, and especially for the purpose of deceiving Congress. The Tonkin incident, where the enemy knew all the facts and the Senate Foreign Relations Committee none, is a case in point.

Of even greater interest is that nearly all decisions in this disastrous enterprise were made in full cognizance of the fact that they probably could not be carried out: hence goals had constantly to be shifted. There are, first, the publicly proclaimed objectives—"seeing that the people of South Vietnam are permitted to determine their future" or "assisting the country to win their contest against the . . . Communist conspiracy" or the containment of China

14

and the avoidance of the domino effect or the protection of America's reputation "as a counter-subversive guarantor."[12] To these Dean Rusk has recently added the aim of preventing World War III, though it seems not to be in the Pentagon papers or to have played a role in the factual record as we know it. The same flexibility marks tactical considerations: North Vietnam is being bombed in order to prevent "a collapse of national morale"[13] in the South and, particularly, the breakdown of the Saigon government. But when the first raids were scheduled to start, the government had broken down, "pandemonium reigned in Saigon," the raids had to be postponed and a new goal found.[14] Now the objective was to compel "Hanoi to stop the Vietcong and the Pathet Lao," an aim that even the Joint Chiefs of Staff did not hope to attain. As they said, "it would be idle to conclude that these efforts will have a decisive effect."[15]

From 1965 on, the notion of a clear-cut victory receded into the background and the objective became "to convince the enemy that *he* could not win" (italics added). Since the enemy remained unconvinced, the next goal appeared: "to avoid a humiliating defeat"—as though the hallmark of a defeat in war were mere humiliation. What the Pentagon papers report is the haunting fear of the impact of defeat, not on the welfare of the nation, but "on the *reputation* of the United States and its President" (italics added). Thus, shortly before, during the many debates about the advisability of using ground troops against North Vietnam, the dominant argument was not fear of defeat itself and con-

12 *The Pentagon Papers,* p. 190.

13 *Ibidem,* p. 312.

14 *Ibidem,* p. 392.

15 *Ibidem,* p. 240.

cern with the welfare of the troops in the case of withdrawal, but: "Once U.S. troops are in, it will be difficult to withdraw them . . . without *admitting* defeat" (italics added).[16] There was, finally, the "political" aim "to show the world the lengths to which the United States will go for a friend" and "to fulfill commitments."[17]

All these goals existed together, in an almost helter-skelter fashion; none was permitted to cancel its predecessors. Each addressed itself to a different "audience," and for each a different "scenario" had to be produced. John T. McNaughton's much-quoted enumeration of U.S. aims in 1965, "70%—To avoid a humiliating U.S. defeat (to our reputation as a guarantor). 20%—To keep SVN [South Vietnam] (and the adjacent) territory from Chinese hands. 10%—To permit the people of SVN to enjoy a better, freer way of life,"[18] is refreshing in its honesty, but was probably drawn up to bring some order and clarity into the debates on the forever troublesome question of why we were conducting a war in Vietnam, of all places. In a previous draft memorandum (1964), McNaughton had shown, perhaps unwittingly, how little he himself, even at that early stage of the bloody game, believed in the attainability of any substantial objectives: "Should South Vietnam disintegrate completely beneath us, we should try to hold it together long enough to permit us to try to evacuate our forces and *to convince the world* to accept the uniqueness (and cogenital impossibility) of the South Vietnamese case" (italics added).[19]

16 *Ibidem,* p. 437.

17 *Ibidem,* pp. 434, 436.

18 *Ibidem,* p. 432.

19 *Ibidem,* p. 368.

"To convince the world"; to "demonstrate that U.S. was a 'good doctor' willing to keep promises, be tough, take risks, get bloodied and hurt the enemy badly";[20] to use a "tiny backward nation" devoid of any strategic importance "as a *test case* of U.S. capacity to help a nation meet a Communist 'war of liberation'" (italics added);[21] to keep intact an image of omnipotence, "our worldwide position of leadership";[22] to demonstrate "the will and the ability of the United States to have its way in world affairs";[23] to show "the credibility of our pledges to friends and allies";[24] in short, to "*behave* like" (italics added) the "greatest power in the world" for no other reason than to convince the world of this "simple fact" (in Walt Rostow's words) [25] —this was the only permanent goal that, with the beginning of the Johnson administration, pushed into the background all other goals and theories, the domino theory and anti-Communist strategy of the initial stages of the Cold War period as well as the counterinsurgency strategy so dear to the Kennedy administration.

The ultimate aim was neither power nor profit. Nor was it even influence in the world in order to serve particular, tangible interests for the sake of which prestige, an image of the "greatest power in the world," was needed and purposefully used. The goal was now the image itself, as is manifest in the very language of the problem-solvers, with their "scenarios" and "audiences," borrowed from the

[20] *Ibidem*, p. 255.

[21] *Ibidem*, p. 278.

[22] *Ibidem*, p. 600.

[23] *Ibidem*, p. 255.

[24] *Ibidem*, p. 600.

[25] *Ibidem*, p. 256.

theater. For this ultimate aim, all policies became short-term interchangeable means, until finally, when all signs pointed to defeat in the war of attrition, the goal was no longer one of avoiding humiliating defeat but of finding ways and means to avoid admitting it and "save face."

Image-making as global policy—not world conquest, but victory in the battle "to win the people's minds"—is indeed something new in the huge arsenal of human follies recorded in history. This was not undertaken by a third-rate nation always apt to boast in order to compensate for the real thing, or by one of the old colonial powers that lost their position as a result of World War II and might have been tempted, as De Gaulle was, to bluff their way back to pre-eminence, but by "the dominant power" at the war's end. It may be natural for elected officeholders—who owe so much, or *believe* they owe so much, to their campaign managers—to think that manipulation is the ruler of the people's minds and hence the true ruler of the world. (The rumor, recently reported in the "Notes and Comment" section of *The New Yorker*, that "the Nixon-Agnew Administration was planning a campaign, organized and directed by Herb Klein, its director of communications, to destroy the 'credibility' of the press before the 1972 Presidential election" is quite in line with this public-relations mentality.) [26]

What is surprising is the eagerness of those scores of "intellectuals" who offered their enthusiastic help in this imaginary enterprise, perhaps because they were fascinated by the sheer size of the mental exercises it seemed to demand. Again, it may be only natural for problem-solvers, trained in translating all factual contents into the language of numbers and percentages, where they can be calculated,

[26] *The New Yorker*, July 10, 1971.

to remain unaware of the untold misery that their "solutions"—pacification and relocation programs, defoliation, napalm, and antipersonnel bullets—held in store for a "friend" who needed to be "saved" and for an "enemy" who had neither the will nor the power to be one before we attacked him. But since they dealt with the people's minds, it remains astonishing that apparently none of them sensed that the "world" might get rather frightened of American friendship and commitment when the "lengths to which the U.S. will go to fulfill" them were "shown" and contemplated.[27] No reality and no common sense could penetrate the minds of the problem-solvers[28] who indefatigably prepared their scenarios for "relevant audiences" in order to change their states of mind—"the Communists (who must feel strong pressures), the South Vietnamese (whose morale must be buoyed), our allies (who must trust us as 'underwriters') and the U.S. public (which must support the risk-taking with U.S. lives and prestige)."[29]

We know today to what extent all these audiences were misjudged; according to Richard J. Barnet, in his excellent contribution to the book *Washington Plans an Aggressive War*, the "war became a disaster because the National Security Managers misjudged each audience."[30] But the greatest, indeed basic, misjudgment was to address audiences with the means of war, to decide military matters from a "political and public-relations perspective"

---

[27] *The Pentagon Papers*, p. 436.

[28] In the words of Leslie H. Gelb: "The foreign-policy community had become a 'house without windows,'" *Life, op. cit.*

[29] *The Pentagon Papers*, p. 438.

[30] In Stavins, Barnet, Raskin, *op. cit.*, p. 209.

(whereby "political" meant the perspective of the next Presidential election and "public relations" the U.S. world image), and to think not about the real risks but of "techniques to minimize the impact of bad outcomes." Among proposals for the latter, the creation of "diversionary 'offensives' elsewhere in the world" was recommended, together with the launching of "an 'anti-poverty' program for underdeveloped areas."[31] Not for a moment did it occur to McNaughton, the author of this memorandum, who doubtless was an unusually intelligent man, that his diversions, unlike the diversions of the theater, would have had grave and totally unpredictable consequences; they would have changed the very world in which the U.S. moved and conducted its war.

It is this remoteness from reality that will haunt the reader of the Pentagon papers who has the patience to stay with them to the end. Barnet, in the essay mentioned above, has this to say on the matter: "The bureaucratic model had completely displaced reality: the hard and stubborn facts, which so many intelligence analysts were paid so much to collect, were ignored."[32] I am not sure that the evils of bureaucracy suffice as an explanation, though they certainly facilitated this defactualization. At any rate, the relation, or, rather, nonrelation, between facts and decision, between the intelligence community and the civilian and military services, is perhaps the most momentous, and certainly the best-guarded, secret that the Pentagon papers revealed.

It would be of great interest to know what enabled the intelligence services to remain so close to reality in this "Alice-in-Wonderland atmosphere," which the papers ascribe to the strange operations of the Saigon government

[31] *The Pentagon Papers,* p. 438.

[32] In Stavins, Barnet, Raskin, *op. cit.,* p. 24.

20

but which seems in retrospect to more aptly describe the defactualized world where political goals were set and military decisions were made. For the beginnings of the role of the services in Southeast Asia were far from promising. Early in *The Pentagon Papers* we find recorded the decision to embark upon "covert warfare" in the early years of the Eisenhower administration, when the executive still believed it needed congressional authority to start a war. Eisenhower was still old-fashioned enough to believe in the Constitution. He met with congressional leaders and decided against open intervention because he was informed that Congress would not support such a decision.[33] When later, beginning with the Kennedy administration, "overt warfare," that is, the dispatching of "combat troops," was discussed, "the question of Congressional authority for open acts of war against a sovereign nation was never seriously raised."[34] Even when, under Johnson, foreign governments were thoroughly briefed on our plans for bombing North Vietnam, similar briefing of and consultation with congressional leaders seem never to have taken place.[35]

During Eisenhower's administration the Saigon Military Mission was formed, under the command of Colonel Edward Lansdale, and told "to undertake paramilitary operations . . . and to wage political-psychological warfare."[36] This meant in practice to print leaflets that would spread lies falsely attributed to the other side, to pour "contaminant in the engines" of the bus company of Hanoi before the French left the North, to conduct an "English-language class . . . for mistresses of important personages," and to

[33] *The Pentagon Papers,* pp. 5 and 11.

[34] *Ibidem,* p. 268.

[35] *Ibidem,* pp. 334–335.

[36] *Ibidem,* p. 16.

hire a team of Vietnamese astrologers.[37] This ludicrous phase continued into the early sixties, until the military took over. After the Kennedy administration, the counterinsurgency doctrine receded into the background—perhaps because, during the overthrow of President Ngo Dinh Diem, it turned out that the C.I.A.-financed Vietnamese Special Forces "had in effect become the private army of Mr. Nhu," Diem's brother and political adviser.[38]

The fact-finding branches of the intelligence services were separated from whatever covert operations were still going on in the field, which meant that they at least were responsible only for gathering information, rather than for creating the news themselves. They had no need to show positive results and were under no pressure from Washington to produce good news to feed into the public-relations machine, or to concoct fairy tales about "continuing progress, virtually miraculous improvement, year in and year out."[39] They were relatively independent, and the result was that they told the truth, year in and year out. It seems that in these intelligence services people did not tell "their superiors what they thought they wanted to hear," that "assessments were [not] made by the implementers," and that no commanding officer told his agents what "an American division commander told one of his district advisers, who insisted on reporting the persistent presence of unpacified Vietcong hamlets in his area: 'Son, you're writing our own report card in this country. Why are you failing us?' "[40] It also seems that those who were responsible

[37] *Ibidem,* p. 15 ff.

[38] *Ibidem,* p. 166.

[39] *Ibidem,* p. 25.

[40] Gelb, in *Foreign Policy, op. cit.;* Ellsberg, *op. cit.*

for intelligence estimates were miles away from the problem-solvers, their disdain for facts, and the accidental character of all facts. The price they paid for these objective advantages was that their reports remained without any influence on the decisions and propositions of the National Security Council.

After 1963, the only discernible trace of the covert-war period is the infamous "provocation strategy," that is, a whole program of "deliberate attempts to provoke the D.R.V. [Democratic Republic of (North) Vietnam] into taking actions which could then be answered by a systematic U.S. air campaign."[41] These tactics do not belong among the ruses of war. They have been typical of the secret police and became notorious as well as counterproductive in the declining days of czarist Russia, when the agents of the Okhrana, by organizing spectacular assassinations, "served despite themselves the ideas of those whom they denounced."[42]

[41] *The Pentagon Papers*, p. 313.

[42] Maurice Laporte, *L'histoire de l'Okhrana*, Paris, 1935, p. 25.

III

THE DIVERGENCE between facts—established by the intelligence services, sometimes by the decision-makers themselves (as notably in the case of McNamara), and often available to the informed public—and the premises, theories, and hypotheses according to which decisions were finally made is total. And the extent of our failures and disasters throughout these years can be grasped only if one has the totality of this divergence firmly in mind. I shall therefore remind the reader of a few outstanding examples.

As regards the domino theory, first enunciated in 1950[43] and permitted to survive, as has been said, the "most momentous events": To the question of President Johnson in 1964, "Would the rest of Southeast Asia necessarily fall if Laos and South Vietnam came under North Vietnamese control?" the C.I.A.'s answer was, "With the possible exception of Cambodia, it is likely that no nation in the area would quickly succumb to Communism as a result of the fall of Laos and South Vietnam."[44] When five years later the Nixon administration raised the same question, it "was advised by the Central Intelligence Agency . . . that [the

[43] *The Pentagon Papers,* p. 6.

[44] *Ibidem,* pp. 253–254.

24

United States] could immediately withdraw from South Vietnam and 'all of Southeast Asia would remain just as it is for at least another generation.' "[45] According to the Pentagon papers, "only the Joint Chiefs, Mr. [Walt W.] Rostow and General [Maxwell] Taylor appear to have accepted the domino theory in its literal sense,"[46] and the point here is that those who did not accept it still used it, not merely for public statements, but as part of their own premises as well.

As to the claim that the insurgents in South Vietnam were "externally directed and supported" by a "Communist conspiracy": The assessment of the intelligence community in 1961 was "that 80-90 per cent of the estimated 17,000 VC had been locally recruited, and that there was little evidence that the VC relied on external supplies."[47] Three years later the situation was unchanged: According to an intelligence analysis of 1964, "the primary sources of Communist strength in South Vietnam are indigenous."[48] In other words, the elementary fact of civil war in South Vietnam was not unknown in the circles of the decision-makers. Had not Senator Mike Mansfield warned Kennedy as early as 1962 that sending more military reinforcements to South Vietnam would mean that "the Americans would be dominating the combat in a civil war . . . [which] would hurt American prestige in Asia and would not help the South Vietnamese to stand on their own two feet, either"?[49]

[45] The Chicago *Sun-Times*, quoted by the New York *Times*, "The Week in Review," June 27, 1971.

[46] *The Pentagon Papers*, p. 254.

[47] *Ibidem*, p. 98.

[48] *Ibidem*, p. 242.

[49] Ellsberg, *op. cit.*, p. 247.

The bombing of North Vietnam nevertheless was begun partly because theory said that "a revolution could be dried up by cutting off external sources of support and supply." The bombings were supposed to "break the will" of North Vietnam to support the rebels in the South, although the decision-makers themselves (in this case McNaughton) knew enough of the indigenous nature of the revolt to doubt that the Viet Cong would "obey a caving" North Vietnam,[50] while the Joint Chiefs did not believe "that these efforts will have a decisive effect" on Hanoi's will to begin with.[51] In 1965, according to a report by McNamara, members of the National Security Council had agreed that North Vietnam "was not likely to quit . . . and in any case, they were more likely to give up because of VC failure in the South than because of bomb-induced 'pain' in the North."[52]

Finally there were, secondary only to the domino theory, the grand stratagems based on the premise of a monolithic Communist world conspiracy and the existence of a Sino-Soviet bloc, in addition to the hypothesis of Chinese expansionism. The notion that China must be "contained" has now, in 1971, been refuted by President Nixon; but more than four years ago McNamara wrote: "To the extent that our original intervention and our existing actions in Vietnam were motivated by the perceived need to draw the line against Chinese expansionism in Asia, our objective has already been attained,"[53] although, only two years earlier, he had agreed that the United States's aim in South

[50] *The Pentagon Papers,* p. 433.

[51] *Ibidem,* p. 240.

[52] *Ibidem,* p. 407.

[53] *Ibidem,* p. 583.

Vietnam was "not to 'help friend' but to contain China."[54]

The war critics have denounced all these theories because of their obvious clash with known facts—such as the nonexistence of a Sino-Soviet bloc, known to everybody familiar with the history of the Chinese revolution and Stalin's resolute opposition to it, or the fragmented character of the Communist movement since the end of World War II. A number of these critics went further and developed a theory of their own: America, having emerged as the greatest power after World War II, has embarked upon a consistent imperialist policy that aims ultimately at world rule. The advantage of this theory was that it could explain the absence of national interest in the whole enterprise— the sign of imperialist aims having always been that they were neither guided nor limited by national interest and territorial boundaries—though it could hardly account for the fact that this country was madly insisting on "pouring its resources down the drain in the wrong place" (as George Ball, Under Secretary of State in the Johnson administration and the only adviser who dared to break the taboo and recommend immediate withdrawal, had the courage to tell the President in 1965).[55]

Clearly this was no case of "limited means to achieve excessive ends."[56] Was it excessive for a "superpower" to add one more small country to its string of client states or to win a victory over a "tiny backward nation"? It was, rather, an unbelievable example of using excessive means to achieve minor aims in a region of marginal interest. It was precisely this unavoidable impression of wrongheaded

[54] *Ibidem,* p. 342.

[55] *Ibidem,* p. 414.

[56] *Ibidem,* p. 584.

floundering that finally brought the country to the conviction "widely and strongly held that 'the Establishment' is out of its mind. The feeling is that we are trying to impose some U.S. image on distant peoples we cannot understand . . . and we are carrying the thing to absurd lengths," as McNaughton wrote in 1967.[57]

At any rate, the Bantam edition of the Pentagon papers contains nothing to support the theory of grandiose imperialist stratagems. Only twice is the importance of land, sea, and air bases, so decisively important for imperialist strategy, mentioned—once by the Joint Chiefs of Staff, who point out that "our ability in limited war" would be "markedly" reduced if a "loss of the Southeast Asian Mainland" resulted in the loss of "air, land and sea bases,"[58] and once in the McNamara report of 1964, which says explicitly: "We do *not* require that it [South Vietnam] serve as a Western base or as a member of a Western Alliance" (italics added).[59] The only public statements of the American government during this period that indeed told almost gospel truth were the often-repeated claims, ever so much less plausible than other public-relations notions, that we were seeking no territorial gains or any other tangible profit.

This is not to say that a genuine American global policy with imperialist overtones would have been impossible after the collapse of the old colonial powers. The Pentagon papers, generally so devoid of spectacular news, reveal one incident, never more than a rumor, so far as I know, that seems to indicate how considerable were the chances for a global policy that was then gambled away in the cause of

[57] *Ibidem,* pp. 534–535.

[58] *Ibidem,* p. 153.

[59] *Ibidem,* p. 278.

image-making and winning people's minds. According to a cable from an American diplomat in Hanoi, Ho Chi Minh wrote several letters in 1945 and 1946 to President Truman requesting the United States "to support the idea of Annamese independence according to the *Philippines example,* to examine the case of the Annamese, and to take steps necessary to maintenance of world peace which is being endangered by French efforts to reconquer Indochina" (italics added).[60] It is true; similar letters were addressed to other countries, China, Russia, and Great Britain, none of which, however, at that particular moment would have been able to give the protection that was requested and that would have established Indochina in the same semiautonomous position as other client states of this country. A second and equally striking incident, apparently mentioned at the time by the Washington *Post*, was recorded in the "Special China Series," documents issued by the State Department in August, 1969, but came to the notice of the public only when reported by Terence Smith in the New York *Times.* Mao and Chou En-lai, it turns out, approached President Roosevelt in January, 1945, "trying to establish relations with the United States in order *to avoid total dependence on the Soviet Union*" (italics added). It seems that Ho Chi Minh never received an answer, and information of the Chinese approach was suppressed because, as Professor Allen Whiting has commented, it contradicted "the image of monolithic Communism directed from Moscow."[61]

Although the decision-makers certainly knew about the

[60] *Ibidem*, pp. 4, 26.

[61] The New York *Times*, June 29, 1971. Mr. Smith cites Professor Whiting's testimony before the Senate Foreign Relations Committee on the document, which appears in *Foreign Relations of the United States: Diplomatic Papers 1945*, Vol. VII: *The Far East, China*, Washington, D.C., 1969, p. 209.

intelligence reports, whose factual statements they had, as it were, to eliminate from their minds day in and day out, I think it entirely possible that they were not aware of these earlier documents, which would have given the lie to all their premises before they could grow into full-blown theory and ruin the country. Certain bizarre circumstances attending the recent irregular and unexpected declassification of top-secret documents point in this direction. It is astounding that the Pentagon papers could have been prepared over years while people in the White House, in the Department of State, and in the Defense Department apparently ignored the study; but it is even more astounding that after its completion, with sets dispatched in all directions within the government bureaucracy, the White House and the State Department were unable even to locate the forty-seven volumes, clearly indicating that those who should have been most concerned with what the study had to tell never set eyes on it.

This sheds some light on one of the gravest dangers of overclassification: not only are the people and their elected representatives denied access to what they must know to form an opinion and make decisions, but also the actors themselves, who receive top clearance to learn all the relevant facts, remain blissfully unaware of them. And this is so not because some invisible hand deliberately leads them astray, but because they work under circumstances, and with habits of mind, that allow them neither time nor inclination to go hunting for pertinent facts in mountains of documents, $99\frac{1}{2}$ per cent of which should not be classified and most of which are irrelevant for all practical purposes. Even now that the press has brought a certain portion of this classified material into the public domain and members of Congress have been given the whole study, it does not look as though those most in need of this information have read it or ever will. At any event, the fact of the matter is that aside from the compilers themselves, "the people who read these documents in the *Times* were the first to study them,"[62] which makes one wonder about the cherished notion that government needs the *arcana imperii* to be able to function properly.

If the mysteries of government have so befogged the minds of the actors themselves that they no longer know or remember the truth behind their concealments and their lies, the whole operation of deception, no matter how well organized its "marathon information campaigns," in Dean Rusk's words, and how sophisticated its Madison Avenue gimmickry, will run aground or become counterproductive, that is, confuse people without convincing them. For the trouble with lying and deceiving is that their efficiency depends entirely upon a clear notion of the truth that the liar and deceiver wishes to hide. In this sense, truth, even if it does not prevail in public, possesses an ineradicable primacy over all falsehoods.

In the case of the Vietnam war we are confronted with, in addition to falsehoods and confusion, a truly amazing and entirely honest ignorance of the historically pertinent background: not only did the decision-makers seem ignorant of all the well-known facts of the Chinese revolution and the decade-old rift between Moscow and Peking that preceded it, but "no one at the top knew or considered it important that the Vietnamese had been fighting foreign invaders for almost 2,000 years,"[63] or that the notion of Vietnam as a "tiny backward nation" without interest to "civilized" nations, which is, unhappily, often shared by the war critics, stands in flagrant contradiction to the very old

[62] Tom Wicker in The New York *Times,* July 8, 1971.

[63] Barnet in Stavins, Barnet, Raskin, *op. cit.,* p. 246.

and highly developed culture of the region. What Vietnam lacks is not "culture," but strategic importance (Indochina is "devoid of decisive military objectives," as a Joint Chiefs of Staff memo said in 1954),[64] a suitable terrain for modern mechanized armies, and rewarding targets for the air force. What caused the disastrous defeat of American policies and armed intervention was indeed no quagmire ("the policy of 'one more step'—each new step always promising the success which the previous *last step* had also *promised* but had unaccountably failed to deliver," in the words of Arthur Schlesinger, Jr., as quoted by Daniel Ellsberg, who rightly denounces the notion as a "myth"),[65] but the willful, deliberate disregard of all facts, historical, political, geographical, for more than twenty-five years.

[64] *The Pentagon Papers,* p. 2.

[65] Ellsberg, *op. cit.,* p. 219.

IV

IF THE quagmire model is a myth and if no grand imperialist stratagems or will to world conquest can be discovered, let alone interest in territorial gains, desire for profit, or, least of all, concern about national security; if, moreover, the reader is disinclined to be satisfied with such general notions as "Greek tragedy" (proposed by Max Frankel and Leslie H. Gelb) or stab-in-the-back legends, always dear to warmongers in defeat, then the question recently raised by Ellsberg, *"How could they?"*[66]—rather than deception and lying per se—will become the basic issue of this dismal story. For the truth, after all, is that the United States was the richest country and the dominant power after the end of World War II, and that today, a mere quarter of a century later, Mr. Nixon's metaphor of the "pitiful, helpless giant" is an uncomfortably apt description of "the mightiest country on earth."

Unable to defeat, with a "1000-to-1 superiority in fire power,"[67] a small nation in six years of overt warfare, unable to take care of its domestic problems and halt the swift decline of its large cities, having wasted its resources

[66] *Ibidem,* p. 235.

[67] Barnet in Stavins, Barnet, Raskin, *op. cit.,* p. 248.

to the point where inflation and currency devaluation threaten its international trade as well as its standard of life at home, the country is in danger of losing much more than its claim to world leadership. And even if one anticipates the judgment of future historians who might see this development in the context of twentieth-century history, when the defeated nations in two world wars managed to come out on top in competition with the victors (chiefly because they were compelled by the victors to rid themselves for a relatively long period of the incredible wastefulness of armaments and military expenses), it remains hard to reconcile oneself to so much effort wasted on demonstrating the impotence of bigness—though one may welcome this unexpected, grand-scale revival of David's triumph over Goliath.

The first explanation that comes to mind to answer the question "How could they?" is likely to point to the interconnectedness of deception and self-deception. In the contest between public statements, always overoptimistic, and the truthful reports of the intelligence community, persistently bleak and ominous, the public statements were liable to win simply because they were public. The great advantage of publicly established and accepted propositions over whatever an individual might secretly know or believe to be the truth is neatly illustrated by a medieval anecdote according to which a sentry, on duty to watch and warn the townspeople of the enemy's approach, jokingly sounded a false alarm—and then was the last to rush to the walls to defend the town against his invented enemies. From this, one may conclude that the more successful a liar is, the more people he has convinced, the more likely it is that he will end by believing his own lies.

In the Pentagon papers we are confronted with people who did their utmost to win the minds of the people, that is, to manipulate them; but since they labored in a free country, where all kinds of information were available, they never really succeeded. Because of their relatively high station and their position in government, they were better shielded—in spite of their privileged knowledge of "top secrets"—against this public information, which also more or less told the factual truth, than were those whom they tried to convince and of whom they were likely to think in terms of mere audiences, "silent majorities," who were supposed to watch the scenarists' productions. The fact that the Pentagon papers revealed hardly any spectacular news testifies to the liars' failure to create a convinced audience that they could then join themselves.

Still, the presence of what Ellsberg has called the process of "internal self-deception"[68] is beyond doubt, but it is as though the normal process of self-deceiving were reversed; it was not as though deception ended with self-deception. The deceivers started with self-deception. Probably because of their high station and their astounding self-assurance, they were so convinced of overwhelming success, not on the battlefield, but in the public-relations arena, and so certain of the soundness of their psychological premises about the unlimited possibilities in manipulating people, that they *anticipated* general belief and victory in the battle for people's minds. And since they lived in a defactualized world anyway, they did not find it difficult to pay no more attention to the fact that their audience refused to be convinced than to other facts.

The internal world of government, with its bureaucracy on one hand, its social life on the other, made self-deception relatively easy. No ivory tower of the scholars has ever better prepared the mind for ignoring the facts of life than

[68] *Op. cit.,* p. 263.

did the various think tanks for the problem-solvers and the reputation of the White House for the President's advisers. It was in this atmosphere, where defeat was less feared than admitting defeat, that the misleading statements about the disasters of the Tet offensive and the Cambodian invasion were concocted. But what is even more important is that the truth about such decisive matters could be successfully covered up in these internal circles—but nowhere else—by worries about how to avoid becoming "the first American President to lose a war" and by the always present preoccupations with the next election.

So far as problem-solving, in contrast to public-relations managing, is concerned, self-deception, even "internal self-deception," is no satisfactory answer to the question "How could they?" Self-deception still presupposes a distinction between truth and falsehood, between fact and fantasy, and therefore a conflict between the real world and the self-deceived deceiver that disappears in an entirely de-factualized world; Washington and its sprawling governmental bureaucracy, as well as the various think tanks in the country, provide the problem-solvers with a natural habitat for mind and body. In the realm of politics, where secrecy and deliberate deception have always played a significant role, self-deception is the danger par excellence; the self-deceived deceiver loses all contact with not only his audience, but also the real world, which still will catch up with him, because he can remove his mind from it but not his body. The problem-solvers who knew all the facts regularly presented to them in the reports of the intelligence community had only to rely on their shared techniques, that is, on the various ways of translating qualities and contents into quantities and numbers with which to calculate outcomes—which then, unaccountably, never came true—in order to eliminate, day in and day out, what they knew to be real. The reason this could work for so many years is precisely that "the goals pursued by the United States government were almost exclusively psychological,"[60] that is, matters of the mind.

Reading the memos, the options, the scenarios, the way percentages are ascribed to the potential risks and returns—"too many risks with too little return"[70]—of contemplated actions, one sometimes has the impression that a computer, rather than "decision-makers," had been let loose in Southeast Asia. The problem-solvers did not *judge;* they calculated. Their self-confidence did not even need self-deception to be sustained in the midst of so many misjudgments, for it relied on the evidence of mathematical, purely rational truth. Except, of course, that this "truth" was entirely irrelevant to the "problem" at hand. If, for instance, it can be calculated that the outcome of a certain action is "less likely to be a general war than more likely,"[71] it does not follow that we can choose it even if the proportion were eighty to twenty, because of the enormity and *incalculable quality* of the risk; and the same is true when the odds of reform in the Saigon government versus the "chance that we would wind up like the French in 1954" are 70 per cent to 30 per cent.[72] That is a nice outlook for a gambler, not for a statesman,[73] and even the gambler would be better advised to take into account what gain or loss would actually mean for him in daily life. Loss may

[69] Barnet in Stavins, Barnet, Raskin, *op. cit.,* p. 209.

[70] *The Pentagon Papers,* p. 576.

[71] *Ibidem,* p. 575.

[72] *Ibidem,* p. 98.

[73] Leslie H. Gelb suggests in all earnestness that the mentality of "our leaders" was formed by "their own careers having been a series of successful gambles, they hoped they somehow could do it again in Vietnam." *Life, op. cit.*

mean utter ruin and gain no more than some welcome but nonessential improvement of his financial affairs. Only if nothing real is at stake for the gambler—a bit more or less money is not likely to make any difference in his standard of life—can he safely rely on the percentage game. The trouble with our conduct of the war in South Vietnam was that no such control, given by reality itself, ever existed in the minds of either the decision-makers or the problem-solvers.

It is indeed true that American policy pursued no real aims, good or bad, that could limit and control sheer fantasy: "Neither territory nor economic advantage has been pursued in Vietnam. The entire purpose of the enormous and costly effect has been to create a specific state of mind."[74] And the reason such excessively costly means, costly in human lives and material resources, were permitted to be used for such politically irrelevant ends must be sought not merely in the unfortunate superabundance in this country, but in its inability to understand that even great power is *limited* power. Behind the constantly repeated cliché of the "mightiest power on earth," there lurked the dangerous myth of omnipotence.

Just as Eisenhower was the last President who knew he would have to request "Congressional authority to commit American troops in Indochina," so his administration was the last to be aware that "the allocation of more than token U.S. armed forces in that area would be a serious diversion of *limited* U.S. capabilities" (italics added).[75] In spite of all the later calculations of "costs, returns and risks" of certain acts, the calculators remained totally unaware of any absolute, nonpsychological limitation. The limits they perceived were the people's minds, how much they would

[74] Barnet in Stavins, Barnet, Raskin, *op. cit.,* p. 209.

[75] *The Pentagon Papers,* pp. 5, 13.

stand in the loss of American lives, which should not be much larger than, for instance, the loss in traffic accidents. But it apparently never occurred to them that there are limits to the resources that even this country can waste without going bankrupt.

This deadly combination of the "arrogance of power"—the pursuit of a mere image of omnipotence, as distinguished from an aim of world conquest, to be attained by nonexistent unlimited resources—with the arrogance of mind, an utterly irrational confidence in the calculability of reality, becomes the leitmotif of the decision-making processes from the beginning of escalation in 1964. This, however, is not to say that the problem-solvers' rigorous methods of defactualization are at the root of this relentless march into self-destruction.

The problem-solvers, who lost their minds because they trusted the calculating powers of their brains at the expense of the mind's capacity for experience and its ability to learn from it, were preceded by the ideologists of the Cold War period. Anti-Communism—not the old, often prejudiced hostility of America against socialism and communism, so strong in the twenties and still a mainstay of the Republican party during the Roosevelt administration, but the postwar comprehensive ideology—was originally the brain child of former Communists who needed a new ideology by which to explain and reliably foretell the course of history. This ideology was at the root of all "theories" in Washington since the end of World War II. I have mentioned the extent to which sheer ignorance of all pertinent facts and deliberate neglect of postwar developments became the hallmark of established doctrine within the establishment. They needed no facts, no information; they had a "theory," and all data that did not fit were denied or ignored.

The methods of this older generation—the methods of

Mr. Rusk as distinguished from those of Mr. McNamara—were less complicated, less brainy, as it were, than those of the problem-solvers, but not less efficacious in shielding men from the impact of reality and in ruining the mind's capacity for judgment and for learning. These men prided themselves on having learned from the past—from Stalin's rule over all Communist parties, hence the notion of "monolithic Communism," and from Hitler's starting a world war after Munich, from which they concluded that every gesture of reconciliation was a "second Munich." They were unable to confront reality on its own terms because they had always some parallels in mind that "helped" them to understand those terms. When Johnson, still in his capacity as Kennedy's Vice-President, came home from an inspection tour in South Vietnam and happily reported that Diem was the "Churchill of Asia," one would have thought that the parallelism game would die from sheer absurdity, but this was not the case. Nor can one say that the left-wing war critics thought in different terms. The extreme fringe had the unhappy inclination of denouncing as "fascist" or "nazi" whatever, often quite rightly, displeased them, and of calling every massacre a genocide, which obviously it was not; this could only help to produce a mentality that was quite willing to condone massacre and other war crimes so long as they were not genocide.

The problem-solvers were remarkably free from the sins of the ideologists; they believed in methods but not in "world views," which, incidentally, is the reason they could be trusted "to pull together the Pentagon's documentary record of the American involvement"[76] in a way that would be both "encyclopedic and objective."[77] But though they

76 *Ibidem,* p. xx.

77 *Ibidem,* p. xviii.

did not believe in such generally accepted rationales for policies as the domino theory, these rationales, with their different methods of defactualization, provided the atmosphere and the background against which the problem-solvers then went to work; they had, after all, to convince the cold warriors, whose minds then turned out to be singularly well prepared for the abstract games they had to offer.

How the cold warriors proceeded when left to themselves is well illustrated by one of the "theories" of Walt Rostow, the Johnson administration's "dominant intellectual." It was Rostow's "theory" that became one of the chief rationales for the decision to bomb North Vietnam against the advice of "McNamara's then prestigious systems analysts in the Defense Department." His theory seemed to have relied on the view of Bernard Fall, one of the most acute observers and best-informed war critics, who had suggested that "Ho Chi Minh *might* disavow the war in the South if some of his new industrial plants were made a target"[78] (italics added). This was a hypothesis, a real possibility, which had to be either confirmed or refuted. But the remark had the ill luck to fit well with Rostow's theories about guerrilla warfare, and was now transformed into a "fact": President Ho Chi Minh "has an industrial complex to protect; he is no longer a guerrilla fighter with nothing to lose."[79] This looks in retrospect, in the eyes of the analyst, like a "colossal misjudgment."[80] But the point is that the "misjudgment" could become "colossal" only because no one wished to correct it in time. It turned out very quickly that the country was not industrialized

[78] Barnet in Stavins, Barnet, Raskin, *op. cit.*, p. 212.

[79] *The Pentagon Papers*, p. 241.

[80] *Ibidem*, p. 469.

enough to suffer from air attacks in a *limited* war whose objective, changing over the years, was never the destruction of the enemy, but, characteristically, "to break his will"; and the government's will in Hanoi, whether or not the North Vietnamese possessed what in Rostow's view was a necessary quality of the guerrilla fighter, refused to be "broken."

To be sure, this failure to distinguish between a plausible hypothesis and the fact that must confirm it, that is, this dealing with hypotheses and mere "theories" as though they were established facts, which became endemic in the psychological and social sciences during the period in question, lacks all the rigor of the methods used by the game theorists and systems analysts. But the source of both —namely, the inability or unwillingness to consult experience and to learn from reality—is the same.

This brings us to the root of the matter that, at least partially, might contain the answer to the question, How could they not only start these policies but carry them through to their bitter and absurd end? Defactualization and problem-solving were welcomed because disregard of reality was inherent in the policies and goals themselves. What did they have to know about Indochina as it really was, when it was no more than a "test case" or a domino, or a means to "contain China" or prove that we *are* the mightiest of the superpowers? Or take the case of bombing North Vietnam for the ulterior purpose of building morale in South Vietnam,[81] without much intention of winning a clear-cut victory and ending the war. How could they be interested in anything as real as victory when they kept the war going not for territorial gain or economic advantage, least of all to help a friend or keep a commitment, and not

[81] *Ibidem,* p. 312.

even for the reality, as distinguished from the image, of power?

When this stage of the game was reached, the initial premise that we should never mind the region or the country itself—inherent in the domino theory—changed into "never mind the enemy." And this in the midst of a war! The result was that the enemy, poor, abused, and suffering, grew stronger while "the mightiest country" grew weaker with each passing year. There are historians today who maintain that Truman dropped the bomb on Hiroshima in order to scare the Russians out of Eastern Europe (with the result we know). If this is true, as it might well be, then we may trace back the earliest beginnings of the disregard for the actual consequences of action in favor of some ulterior calculated aim to the fateful war crime that ended the last world war. The Truman Doctrine, at any rate, "depicted a world full of dominoes," as Leslie H. Gelb has pointed out.

V

AT THE BEGINNING of this analysis I tried to suggest that the aspects of the Pentagon papers that I have chosen, the aspects of deception, self-deception, image-making, ideologizing, and defactualization, are by no means the only features of the papers that deserve to be studied and learned from. There is, for instance, the fact that this massive and systematic effort at self-examination was commissioned by one of the chief actors, that thirty-six men could be found to compile the documents and write their analysis, quite a few of whom "had helped to develop or to carry out the policies they were asked to evaluate,"[82] that one of the authors, when it had become apparent that no one in government was willing to use or even to read the results, went to the public and leaked it to the press, and that, finally, the most respectable newspapers in the country dared to bring material that was stamped "top secret" to the widest possible attention. It has rightly been said by Neil Sheehan that Robert McNamara's decision to find out what went wrong, and why, "may turn out to be one of the most important decisions in his seven years at the Pentagon."[83] It certainly restored, at least for a fleeting moment,

[82] *Ibidem,* p. xviii.

[83] *Ibidem,* p. ix.

this country's reputation in the world. What had happened could indeed hardly have happened anywhere else. It is as though all these people, involved in an unjust war and rightly compromised by it, had suddenly remembered what they owed to their forefathers' "decent respect for the opinions of mankind."

What calls for further close and detailed study is the fact, much commented on, that the Pentagon papers revealed little significant news that was not available to the average reader of dailies and weeklies; nor are there any arguments, pro or con, in the "History of U.S. Decision-Making Process on Vietnam Policy" that have not been debated publicly for years in magazines, television shows, and radio broadcasts. (Personal positions and changes in them aside, the different views of the intelligence community on basic issues were the only matter generally unknown.) That the public had access for years to material that the government vainly tried to keep from it testifies to the integrity and to the power of the press even more forcefully than the way the *Times* broke the story. What has often been suggested has now been established: so long as the press is free and not corrupt, it has an enormously important function to fulfill and can rightly be called the fourth branch of government. Whether the First Amendment will suffice to protect this most essential political freedom, the right to unmanipulated factual information without which all freedom of opinion becomes a cruel hoax, is another question.

There is, finally, a lesson to be learned by those who, like myself, believed that this country had embarked on an imperialist policy, had utterly forgotten its old anticolonial sentiments, and was perhaps succeeding in establishing that Pax Americana that President Kennedy had denounced. Whatever the merits of these suspicions, and they could be justified by our policies in Latin America, if undeclared small wars—aggressive brush-fire operations in foreign lands—are among the necessary means to attain imperialist ends, the United States will be less able to employ them successfully than almost any other great power. For while the demoralization of American troops has by now reached unprecedented proportions—according to *Der Spiegel*, during the past year 89,088 deserters, 100,-000 conscientious objectors, and tens of thousands of drug addicts[84]—the disintegration process of the army started much earlier and was preceded by similar developments during the Korean War.[85] One has only to talk to a few of the veterans of this war—or to read Daniel Lang's sober and telling report in *The New Yorker*[86] about the development of a fairly typical case—to realize that in order for this country to carry adventurous and aggressive policies to success there would have to be a decisive change in the American people's "national character." The same could of course be concluded from the extraordinarily strong, highly qualified, and well-organized opposition that has from time to time arisen at home. The North Vietnamese who watched these developments carefully over the years had their hopes always set on them, and it seems that they were right in their assessment.

No doubt all this can change. But one thing has become clear in recent months: the halfhearted attempts of the government to circumvent Constitutional guarantees and to intimidate those who have made up their minds not to be intimidated, who would rather go to jail than see their liberties nibbled away, are not enough and probably

[84] *Der Spiegel*, Number 35, 1971.

[85] Eugene Kinkead, "Reporter at Large," *The New Yorker*, October 26, 1957.

[86] *The New Yorker*, September 4, 1971.

will not be enough to destroy the Republic. There is reason to hope, with Mr. Lang's veteran—one of the nation's two and a half million—"that the country might regain its better side as a result of the war. 'I know it's nothing to bet on,' he said, 'but neither is anything else I can think of.' "[87]

[87] *Ibidem.*

Civil Disobedience

IN THE SPRING of 1970, the Bar Association of the City of New York celebrated its centennial with a symposium on the rather dismal question "Is the law dead?" It would be interesting to know what precisely inspired this cry of despair. Was it the disastrous increase in crime in the streets or was it the farther-reaching insight that "the enormity of evil expressed in modern tyrannies has undermined any simple faith in the central importance of fidelity to law" in addition to "ample evidence that skillfully organized campaigns of civil disobedience can be very effective in securing desirable changes in the law"?[1] The topics, at any event, on which participants were asked by Eugene V. Rostow to prepare their papers clearly encouraged a somewhat brighter outlook. One of them proposed a discussion of "the citizen's moral relation to the law in a society of consent," and the following remarks are in answer to this. The literature on the subject relies to large extent on two famous men in prison—Socrates, in Athens, and Thoreau, in Concord. Their conduct is the joy of jurists because it seems to prove that disobedience to the law can

[1] See Graham Hughes, "Civil Disobedience and the Political Question Doctrine," in *New York University Law Review*, 43:2 (March, 1968).

be justified only if the lawbreaker is willing and even eager to accept punishment for his act. There are few who would not agree with Senator Philip A. Hart's position: "Any tolerance that I might feel toward the disobeyer is dependent on his willingness to accept whatever punishment the law might impose."[2] This argument harks back to the popular understanding, and perhaps misunderstanding, of Socrates, but its plausibility in this country seems to be greatly strengthened by "one of the most serious oddities of our law [through which an individual] is encouraged or in some sense compelled to establish a significant legal right through a personal act of civil disobedience."[3] This oddity has given rise to a strange and, as we shall see, not altogether happy theoretical marriage of morality and legality, conscience and the law of the land.

[2] In *To Establish Justice, to Insure Domestic Tranquility,* Final Report of the National Commission on the Causes and the Prevention of Violence, December, 1969, p. 108. For the use of Socrates and Thoreau in these discussions, see also Eugene V. Rostow, "The Consent of the Governed," in *The Virginia Quarterly,* Autumn, 1968.

[3] Thus Edward H. Levi in "The Crisis in the Nature of Law," in The Record of the Association of the Bar of the City of New York, March, 1970. Mr. Rostow, on the contrary, holds that "it is a common error to think of such breaches of the law as acts of disobedience to law" (*op. cit.*), and Wilson Carey McWilliams in one of the most interesting essays on the subject—"Civil Disobedience and Contemporary Constitutionalism," in *Comparative Politics,* vol. I, 1969—seems to agree by implication. Stressing that the court's "tasks depend, in part, on public action," he concludes: "The Court acts, in fact, to authorize disobedience to otherwise legitimate authority, and it depends on citizens who will take advantage of its authorizations" (p. 216). I fail to see how this can remedy Mr Levi's "oddity"; the lawbreaking citizen who wishes to persuade the courts to pass on the constitutionality of some statute must be willing to pay the price like any other lawbreaker for the act—either until the court has decided the case or if it should decide against him.

Because "our dual system of law permits the possibility that state law will be inconsistent with federal law,"[4] the civil-rights movement in its early stages, though clearly in disobedience to ordinances as well as laws of the South, could indeed be understood to have done no more than "to appeal, in our federal system, over the head of the law and the authority of the state, to the law and authority of the nation"; there was, we are told—a hundred years of nonenforcement notwithstanding—"not the faintest real doubt that the [states'] ordinances were void under federal law" and that "the defiance of the law was all on the other side."[5] At first glance, the merits of this construction seem considerable. The jurist's chief difficulty in construing a compatibility of civil disobedience with the legal system of the country, namely, that "the law cannot justify the breaking of the law,"[6] seems ingeniously solved by the duality of American law and the identification of civil disobedience with the violation of a law for the purpose of testing its constitutionality. There is also the added advantage, or so it seems, that because of its dual system American law, in distinction from other legal systems, has found a nonfictitious, visible place for that "higher law" on which "in one form or another jurisprudence keeps insisting."[7]

It would require quite a bit of ingenuity to defend this

[4] Nicholas W. Puner, "Civil Disobedience: An Analysis and Rationale" in *New York University Law Review*, 43:714 (October, 1968).

[5] Charles L. Black, "The Problem of the Compatibility of Civil Disobedience with American Institutions of Government," in *Texas Law Review*, 43:496 (March, 1965).

[6] See, in the special issue of the *Rutgers Law Review* (vol. 21, Fall, 1966) on "Civil Disobedience and the Law," Carl Cohen, p. 8.

[7] *Ibid.*, Harrop A. Freeman, p. 25.

doctrine on theoretical grounds: the situation of the man who tests the legitimacy of a law by breaking it is "only marginally, if at all, one of civil disobedience";[8] and the disobeyer who acts on strong moral conviction and appeals to a "higher law" will find it rather strange if he is asked to recognize the various decisions of the Supreme Court over the centuries as inspired by that law above all laws whose chief characteristic is its immutability. On factual grounds, at any rate, the doctrine was refuted when the civil disobedients of the civil-rights movement smoothly developed into the resisters of the antiwar movement who clearly disobeyed federal law, and this refutation became final when the Supreme Court refused to rule on the legality of the war in Vietnam because of "the political question doctrine," that is, precisely for the same reason that unconstitutional laws had been tolerated without the slightest impediment for such a long time.

Meanwhile, the number of civil disobedients or potential civil disobedients—that is, of people who volunteered for demonstration duty in Washington—has steadily increased, and with it the inclination of the government either to treat the protesters as common criminals or to demand the supreme proof of "self-sacrifice": the disobedient who has violated valid law should "welcome his punishment." (Harrop A. Freeman has nicely pointed to the absurdity of this demand from a lawyer's point of view: "No lawyer goes into court and says, 'Your Honor, this man wants to be punished.' "[9]) And the insistence on

[8] See Graham Hughes, *op. cit.,* p. 4.

[9] *Rutgers Law Review, op. cit.,* p. 26, where Freeman argues against the opinion of Carl Cohen: "Because the civil disobedient acts within a framework of laws whose legitimacy he accepts, this legal punishment is more than a possible consequence of his act—it is the

this unfortunate and inadequate alternative is perhaps only natural "in a period of turmoil," when "the distinction between such acts [in which an individual breaks the law in order to test its constitutionality] and ordinary violations becomes much more fragile," and when, not local laws, but "the national lawmaking power" is being challenged.[10]

Whatever the actual causes of the period of turmoil—and they are of course factual and political ones—the present confusion, polarization, and growing bitterness of our debates are also caused by a theoretical failure to come to terms with and to understand the true character of the phenomenon. Whenever the jurists attempt to justify the civil disobedient on moral and legal grounds, they construe his case in the image of either the conscientious objector or the man who tests the constitutionality of a statute. The trouble is that the situation of the civil disobedient bears no analogy to either for the simple reason that he never exists as a single individual; he can function and survive only as a member of a group. This is seldom admitted, and even in these rare instances only marginally mentioned; "civil disobedience practiced by a single individual is unlikely to have much effect. He will be regarded as an eccentric more interesting to observe than to suppress. Significant civil disobedience, therefore, will be practiced by a number of people who have a community of interest."[11] Yet one of the chief characteristics of the

---

natural and proper culmination of it. . . . He thereby demonstrates his willingness even to sacrifice himself in behalf of that cause" (*ibid.*, p. 6).

[10] See Edward H. Levi, *op. cit.*, and Nicholas W. Puner, *op. cit.*, p. 702.

[11] Nicholas W. Puner, *op. cit.*, p. 714.

act itself—conspicuous already in the case of the Freedom Riders—namely, "indirect disobedience," where laws (for instance, traffic regulations) are violated that the disobedient regards as nonobjectionable in themselves in order to protest unjust ordinances or governmental policies and executive orders, presupposes a group action (imagine a single individual disregarding traffic laws!) and has rightly been called disobedience "in the strict sense."[12]

It is precisely this "indirect disobedience," which would make no sense whatsoever in the case of the conscientious objector or the man who breaks a specific law to test its constitutionality, that seems legally unjustifiable. Hence, we must distinguish between conscientious objectors and civil disobedients. The latter are in fact organized minorities, bound together by common opinion, rather than by common interest, and the decision to take a stand against the government's policies even if they have reason to assume that these policies are backed by a majority; their concerted action springs from an agreement with each other, and it is this agreement that lends credence and conviction to their opinion, no matter how they may originally have arrived at it. Arguments raised in defense of individual conscience or individual acts, that is, moral imperatives and appeals to a "higher law," be it secular or transcendent,[13] are inadequate when applied to civil dis-

[12] Marshall Cohen, "Civil Disobedience in a Constitutional Democracy," in *The Massachusetts Review*, 10:211-226, Spring, 1969.

[13] Norman Cousins has set forth a series of steps in which the concept of a purely secular higher law would function:
"If there is a conflict between the security of the sovereign state and the security of the human commonwealth, the human commonwealth comes first.
"If there is a conflict between the well-being of the nation and the well-being of mankind, the well-being of mankind comes first.

obedience; on this level, it will be not only "difficult," but impossible "to keep civil disobedience from being a philosophy of subjectivity . . . intensely and exclusively personal, so that any individual, for whatever reason, can disobey."[14]

"If there is a conflict between the needs of this generation and the needs of later generations, the needs of the later generations come first.

"If there is a conflict between the rights of the state and the rights of man, the rights of man come first. The state justifies its existence only as it serves and safeguards the rights of man.

"If there is a conflict between public edict and private conscience, private conscience comes first.

"If there is a conflict between the easy drift of prosperity and the ordeal of peace, the ordeal of peace comes first." (*A Matter of Life,* 1963, pp. 83-84; cited in *Rutgers Law Review, op. cit.,* p. 26.)

I find it rather difficult to be convinced of this understanding of higher law "in terms of first principles," as Cousins thinks of his enumeration.

[14] Nicholas W. Puner, *op. cit.,* p. 708.

I

THE IMAGES of Socrates and Thoreau occur not only in the literature on our subject, but also, and more importantly, in the minds of the civil disobedients themselves. To those who were brought up in the Western tradition of conscience—and who was not?—it seems only natural to think of their agreement with others as secondary to a solitary decision *in foro conscientiae,* as though what they had in common with others was not an opinion or a judgment at all, but a common conscience. And since the arguments used to buttress this position are usually suggested by more or less vague reminiscences of what Socrates or Thoreau had to say about the "citizen's moral relation to the law," it may be best to begin these considerations with a brief examination of what these two men actually had to say on the matter.

As for Socrates, the decisive text is, of course, Plato's *Crito,* and the arguments presented there are much less unequivocal and certainly less useful for the demand of cheerful submission to punishment than the legal and philosophical textbooks tell us. There is first the fact that Socrates, during his trial, never challenged the laws themselves—only this particular miscarriage of justice, which he spoke of as the "accident" ($\tau \acute{v} \chi \eta$) that had befallen him.

His personal misfortune did not entitle him to "break his contracts and agreements" with the laws; his quarrel was not with the laws, but with the judges. Moreover, as Socrates pointed out to Crito (who tried to persuade him to escape and go into exile), at the time of the trial the laws themselves had offered him this choice: "At that time you could have done with the state's consent what you are trying now to do without it. But then you gloried in being willing to die. You said that you preferred death to exile" (52). We also know, from the *Apology*, that he had the option of desisting from his public examination of things, which doubtless spread uncertainty about established customs and beliefs, and that again he had preferred death, because "an unexamined life is not worth living." That is, Socrates would not have honored his own words if he had tried to escape; he would have undone all he had done during his trial—would have "confirmed the judges in their opinion, and made it seem that their verdict was a just one" (53). He owed it *to himself*, as well as to the citizens he had addressed, to stay and die. "It is the payment of a debt of honor, the payment of a gentleman who has lost a wager and who pays because he cannot otherwise live with himself. There has indeed been a contract, and the notion of a contract pervades the latter half of the *Crito*, but . . . the contract which is binding is . . . *the commitment involved in the trial*" (my italics).[15]

Thoreau's case, though much less dramatic (he spent one night in jail for refusing to pay his poll tax to a government that permitted slavery, but he let his aunt pay it

---

[15] See N. A. Greenberg's excellent analysis, "Socrates' Choice in the *Crito*" (*Harvard Studies in Classical Philology*, vol. 70, no. 1, 1965), which proved that the *Crito* can be understood only if read in conjunction with the *Apology*.

for him the next morning), seems at first glance more pertinent to our current debates, for, in contradistinction to Socrates, he protested against the injustice of the laws themselves. The trouble with this example is that in "On the Duty of Civil Disobedience," the famous essay that grew out of the incident and made the term "civil disobedience" part of our political vocabulary, he argued his case not on the ground of a *citizen's* moral relation to the law, but on the ground of individual conscience and conscience's moral obligation: "It is not a man's duty, as a matter of course, to devote himself to the eradication of any, even the most enormous, wrong; he may still properly have other concerns to engage him; but it is his duty, at least, to wash his hands of it, and, if he gives it no thought longer, not to give it practically his support." Thoreau did not pretend that a man's washing his hands of it would make the world better or that a man had any obligation to do so. He "came into this world not chiefly to make this a good place to live in, but to live in it, be it good or bad." Indeed, this is how we all come into the world—lucky if the world and the part of it we arrive in is a good place to live in at the time of our arrival, or at least a place where the wrongs committed are not "of such a nature that it requires you to be the agent of injustice to another." For only if this is the case, "then, I say, break the law." And Thoreau was right: individual conscience requires nothing more.[16]

Here, as elsewhere, conscience is unpolitical. It is not primarily interested in the world where the wrong is committed or in the consequences that the wrong will have for the future course of the world. It does not say, with

[16] All quotations are from Thoreau's "On the Duty of Civil Disobedience" (1849).

Jefferson, "I tremble *for my country* when I reflect that God is just; that His justice cannot sleep forever,"[17] because it trembles for the individual self and its integrity. It can therefore be much more radical and say, with Thoreau, "This people must cease to hold slaves, and to make war on Mexico, *though it cost them their existence as a people*" (italics added), whereas for Lincoln "the paramount object," even in the struggle for the emancipation of the slaves, remained, as he wrote in 1862, "to save the Union, and . . . not either to save or destroy slavery."[18] This does not mean that Lincoln was unaware of "the monstrous injustice of slavery itself," as he had called it eight years earlier; it means that he was also aware of the distinction between his "official duty" and his "personal wish that all men everywhere could be free."[19] And this distinction, if one strips it of the always complex and equivocal historical circumstances, is ultimately the same as Machiavelli's when he said, "I love my native city more than my own soul."[20] The discrepancy between "official duty" and "personal wish" in Lincoln's case no more indicates a lack of moral commitment than the discrepancy between city and soul indicates that Machiavelli was an atheist and did not believe in eternal salvation and damnation.

This possible conflict between "the good man" and "the

---

[17] *Notes on the State of Virginia,* Query XVIII (1781-85).

[18] In his famous letter to Horace Greeley, quoted here from Hans Morgenthau, *The Dilemmas of Politics,* Chicago, 1958, p. 80.

[19] Quoted from Richard Hofstadter, *The American Political Tradition,* New York, 1948, p. 110.

[20] Allan Gilbert, ed., *The Letters of Machiavelli,* New York, 1961, letter 225.

good citizen" (according to Aristotle, the good man could be a good citizen only in a good state; according to Kant, even "a race of devils" could solve successfully the problem of establishing a constitution, "if only they are intelligent"), between the individual self, with or without belief in an afterlife, and the member of the community, or, as we would say today, between morality and politics, is very old—older, even, than the word "conscience," which in its present connotation is of relatively recent origin. And almost equally old are the justifications for the position of either. Thoreau was consistent enough to recognize and admit that he was open to the charge of irresponsibility, the oldest charge against "the good man." He said explicitly that he was "not responsible for the successful working of the machinery of society," was "not the son of the engineer." The adage *Fiat justicia et pereat mundus* (Let justice be done even if the world perishes), which is usually invoked rhetorically against the defenders of absolute justice, often for the purpose of excusing wrongs and crimes, neatly expresses the gist of the dilemma.

However, the reason that "at the level of individual morality, the problem of disobedience to the law is wholly intractable"[21] is of still a different order. The counsels of conscience are not only unpolitical; they are always expressed in purely subjective statements. When Socrates stated that "it is better to suffer wrong than to do wrong," he clearly meant that it was better *for him,* just as it was better for him "to be in disagreement with multitudes than, being one, to be in disagreement with [himself]."[22] Politically, on the contrary, what counts is that a wrong has been done; to the law it is irrelevant who is better off

[21] *To Establish Justice . . . , op. cit.,* p. 98.

[22] *Gorgias,* 482 and 489.

as a result—the doer or the sufferer. Our legal codes distinguish between crimes in which indictment is mandatory, because the community as a whole has been violated, and offenses in which only doers and sufferers are involved, who may or may not want to sue. In the case of the former, the states of mind of those involved are irrelevant, except insofar as intent is part of the overt act, or mitigating circumstances are taken into account; it makes no difference whether the one who suffered is willing to forgive or the one who did is entirely unlikely to do it again.

In the *Gorgias*, Socrates does not address the citizens, as he does in the *Apology* and, in support of the *Apology*, in the *Crito*. Here Plato lets Socrates speak as the philosopher who has discovered that men have intercourse not only with their fellow men but also with themselves, and that the latter form of intercourse—my being with and by myself—prescribes certain rules for the former. These are the rules of conscience, and they are—like those Thoreau announced in his essay—entirely negative. They do not say what to do; they say what not to do. They do not spell out certain principles for taking action; they lay down boundaries no act should transgress. They say: Don't do wrong, for then you will have to live together with a wrongdoer. Plato, in the later dialogues (the *Sophist* and the *Theaetetus*), elaborated on this Socratic intercourse of me with myself and defined thinking as the soundless dialogue between me and myself; existentially speaking, this dialogue, like all dialogues, requires that the partners be friends. The validity of the Socratic propositions depends upon the kind of man who utters them and the kind of man to whom they are addressed. They are self-evident truths for man insofar as he is a thinking being; to those who don't think, who don't have intercourse with themselves, they are not self-evident, nor can they be proved.[23] Those men—and they are the "multitudes"—can gain a proper interest in themselves only, according to Plato, by believing in a mythical hereafter with rewards and punishments.

Hence, the rules of conscience hinge on interest in the self. They say: Beware of doing something that you will not be able to live with. It is the same argument that led to "Camus's . . . stress on the necessity of resistance to injustice *for the resisting individual's own health and welfare*" (my italics).[24] The political and legal trouble with such justification is twofold. First, it cannot be generalized; in order to keep its validity, it must remain subjective. What I cannot live with may not bother another man's conscience. The result is that conscience will stand against conscience. "If the decision to break the law really turned on individual conscience, it is hard to see in law how Dr. King is better off than Governor Ross Barnett, of Mississippi, who also believed deeply in his cause and was willing to go to jail."[25] The second, and perhaps even more serious, trouble is that conscience, if it is defined in secular terms, presupposes not only that man possesses the innate faculty of telling right from wrong, but also that man is interested in himself, for the obligation arises from

[23] This is made quite clear in the second book of the *Republic*, where Socrates' own pupils "can plead the cause of injustice most eloquently and still not be convinced themselves" (357-367). They are and remain convinced of justice as a self-evident truth, but Socrates' arguments are not convincing and they show that with this kind of reasoning the cause of injustice can just as well be "proved."

[24] Quoted by Christian Bay, "Civil Disobedience," in the *International Encyclopedia of the Social Sciences*, 1968, II, 486.

[25] *To Establish Justice* . . . , *op. cit.*, p. 99.

this interest alone. And this kind of self-interest can hardly be taken for granted. Although we know that human beings are capable of thinking—of having intercourse with themselves—we do not know how many indulge in this rather profitless enterprise; all we can say is that the habit of thinking, of reflecting on what one is doing, is independent of the individual's social, educational, or intellectual standing. In this respect, as in so many others, "the good man" and "the good citizen" are by no means the same, and not only in the Aristotelian sense. Good men become manifest only in emergencies, when they suddenly appear, as if from nowhere, in all social strata. The good citizen, on the contrary, must be conspicuous; he can be studied, with the not so very comforting result that he turns out to belong to a small minority: he tends to be educated and a member of the upper social classes.[26]

This whole question of the political weight to be accorded moral decisions—decisions arrived at *in foro conscientiae*—has been greatly complicated by the originally religious and later secularized associations that the notion of conscience acquired under the influence of Christian philosophy. As we use the word today, in both moral and legal matters, conscience is supposed to be always present within us, as though it were identical with consciousness. (It is true that it took language a long time to distinguish between the two, and in some languages—French, for instance—the separation of conscience and consciousness has never taken place.) The voice of conscience was the voice of God, and announced the Divine Law, before it became the *lumen naturale* that informed men of a higher law. As the voice of God, it gave positive prescriptions whose validity rested on the command "Obey God rather than

26 Wilson Carey McWilliams, *op. cit.*, p. 223.

men"—a command that was objectively binding without any reference to human institutions and that could be turned, as in the Reformation, even against what was alleged to be the divinely inspired institution of the Church. To modern ears, this must sound like "self-certification," which "borders on blasphemy"—the presumptuous pretension that one knows the will of God and is sure of his eventual justification.[27] It did not sound that way to the believer in a creator God who has revealed Himself to the one creature He created in His own image. But the anarchic nature of divinely inspired consciences, so blatantly manifest in the beginnings of Christianity, cannot be denied.

The law, therefore—rather late, and by no means in all countries—recognized religiously inspired conscientious objectors but recognized them only when they appealed to a Divine Law that was also claimed by a recognized religious group, which could not well be ignored by a Christian community. The present deep crisis in the churches and the increasing number of objectors who claim no relation to any religious institution, whether or not they claim divinely informed consciences, have thus created great difficulties. These difficulties are not likely to be dissolved by substituting the submission to punishment for the appeal to a publicly recognized and religiously sanctioned higher law. "The idea that paying the penalty justifies breaking the law derives, not from Gandhi and the tradition of civil disobedience, but from Oliver Wendell Holmes and the tradition of legal realism. . . . This doctrine . . . is plainly absurd . . . in the area of

27 Thus Leslie Dunbar, as quoted in "On Civil Disobedience in Recent American Democratic Thought," by Paul F. Power, in *The American Political Science Review*, March, 1970.

criminal law. . . . It is mindless to suppose that murder, rape or arson would be justified if only one were willing to pay the penalty."[28] It is most unfortunate that, in the eyes of many, a "self-sacrificial element" is the best proof of "intensity of concern,"[29] of "the disobedient's seriousness and his fidelity to law,"[30] for single-minded fanaticism is usually the hallmark of the crackpot and, in any case, makes impossible a rational discussion of the issues at stake.

Moreover, the conscience of the believer who listens to and obeys the voice of God or the commands of the *lumen naturale* is a far cry from the strictly secular conscience—this knowing, and speaking with, myself, which, in Ciceronian language, better than a thousand witnesses testifies to deeds that otherwise may remain unknown forever. It is this conscience that we find in such magnificence in *Richard III*. It does no more than "fill a man full of obstacles"; it is not always with him but awaits him when he is alone, and loses its hold when midnight is over and he has rejoined the company of his peers. Then only, when he is no longer by himself, will he say, "Conscience is but a word that cowards use,/Devised at first to keep the strong in awe." The fear of being alone and having to face oneself can be a very effective dissuader from wrongdoing, but this fear, by its very nature, is unpersuasive of others. No doubt even this kind of conscientious objection can become politically significant when a number of consciences happen to coincide, and the conscientious objectors decide to enter the market place and make their voices heard in

[28] Marshall Cohen, *op. cit.*, p. 214.

[29] Carl Cohen, *op. cit.*, p. 6.

[30] Thus Marshall Cohen, *op. cit.*

public. But then we are no longer dealing with individuals, or with a phenomenon whose criteria can be derived from Socrates or Thoreau. What had been decided *in foro conscientiae* has now become part of public opinion, and although this particular group of civil disobedients may still claim the initial validation—their consciences—they actually rely no longer on themselves alone. In the market place, the fate of conscience is not much different from the fate of the philosopher's truth: it becomes an opinion, indistinguishable from other opinions. And the strength of opinion does not depend on conscience, but on the number of those with whom it is associated—"unanimous agreement that 'X' is an evil . . . adds credence to the belief that 'X' *is* an evil."[31]

[31] Nicholas W. Puner, *op. cit.*, p. 714.

II

DISOBEDIENCE to the law, civil and criminal, has become a mass phenomenon in recent years, not only in America, but also in a great many other parts of the world. The defiance of established authority, religious and secular, social and political, as a world-wide phenomenon may well one day be accounted the outstanding event of the last decade. Indeed, "the laws seem to have lost their power."[32] Viewed from the outside and considered in historical perspective, no clearer writing on the wall—no more explicit sign of the inner instability and vulnerability of existing governments and legal systems—could be imagined. If history teaches anything about the causes of revolution—and history does not teach much, but still teaches considerably more than social-science theories—it is that a disintegration of political systems precedes revolutions, that the telling symptom of disintegration is a progressive erosion of governmental authority, and that this erosion is caused by the government's inability to function properly, from which spring the citizens' doubts about its legitimacy. This is what the Marxists used to call a "rev-

[32] Wilson Carey McWilliams, *op. cit.*, p. 211.

69

olutionary situation"—which, of course, more often than not does not develop into a revolution.

In our context, the grave threat to the judicial system of the United States is a case in point. To lament "the cancerous growth of disobediences"[33] does not make much sense unless one recognizes that for many years now the law-enforcement agencies have been unable to enforce the statutes against drug traffic, mugging, and burglary. Considering that the chances that criminal offenders in these categories will never be detected at all are better than nine to one and that only one in a hundred will ever go to jail, there is every reason to be surprised that such crime is not worse than it is. (According to the 1967 report of the President's Commission on Law Enforcement and Administration of Justice, "well over half of all crimes are never reported to the police," and "of those which are, fewer than one-quarter are cleared by arrest. Nearly half of all arrests result in the dismissal of charges.")[34] It is as though we were engaged in a nationwide experiment to find out how many potential criminals—that is, people who are prevented from committing crimes only by the deterrent force of the law—actually exist in a given society. The results may not be encouraging to those who hold that all criminal impulses are aberrations—that is, are the impulses of mentally sick people acting under the compulsion of their illness. The simple and rather frightening truth is that under circumstances of legal and social permissiveness people will engage in the most outrageous criminal behavior who under normal circumstances per-

---

[33] *To Establish Justice . . . op. cit.,* p. 89.

[34] *Law and Order Reconsidered,* Report of the Task Force on Law and Law Enforcement to the National Commission on the Causes and Prevention of Violence. n.d., p. 266.

70

haps dreamed of such crimes but never considered actually committing them.[35]

In today's society, neither potential lawbreakers (that is, nonprofessional and unorganized criminals) nor law-abiding citizens need elaborate studies to tell them that criminal acts will probably—which is to say, predictably—have no legal consequences whatsoever. We have learned, to our sorrow, that organized crime is less to be feared than nonprofessional hoodlums—who profit from opportunity—and their entirely justified "lack of concern about being punished"; and this state of affairs is neither altered nor clarified by research into the "public's confidence in American judicial process."[36] What we are up against is not the judi-

[35] Horrible examples of this truth were presented during the so-called "Auschwitz trial" in Germany, for whose proceedings see Bernd Naumann, *Auschwitz*, New York, 1966. The defendants were "a mere handful of intolerable cases," selected from about 2,000 S.S. men posted at the camp between 1940 and 1945. All of them were charged with murder, the only offense which in 1963, when the trial began, was not covered by the statute of limitations. Auschwitz was the camp of systematic extermination, but the atrocities almost all the accused had committed had nothing do with the order for the "final solution"; their crimes were punishable under Nazi law, and in rare cases such perpetrators were actually punished by the Nazi government. These defendants had not been specially selected for duty at an extermination camp; they had come to Auschwitz for no other reason than that they were unfit for military service. Hardly any of them had a criminal record of any sort, and none of them a record of sadism and murder. Before they had come to Auschwitz and during the eighteen years they had lived in postwar Germany, they had been respectable and respected citizens, undistinguishable from their neighbors.

[36] The allusion is to the million-dollar grant made by the Ford Foundation "for studies of the public's confidence in the American judicial process," in contrast to the "survey of law-enforcement officials" by Fred P. Graham, of the New York *Times,* which, with no

cial process, but the simple fact that criminal acts usually have no legal consequences whatsoever; they are not followed by judicial process. On the other hand, one must ask what would happen if police power were restored to the reasonable point where from 60 to 70 per cent of all criminal offenses were properly cleared by arrest and properly judged. Is there any doubt that it would mean the collapse of the already disastrously overburdened courts and would have quite terrifying consequences for the just as badly overloaded prison system? What is so frightening in the present situation is not only the failure of police power per se, but also that to remedy this condition radically would spell disaster for these other, equally important branches of the judicial system.

The answer of the government to this, and to similarly obvious breakdowns of public services, has invariably been the creation of study commissions, whose fantastic proliferation in recent years has probably made the United States the most researched country on earth. No doubt the commissions, after spending much time and money in order to find out that "the poorer you are, the more likely you are to suffer from serious malnutrition" (a piece of wisdom that even made the New York *Times*'s "Quotation of the Day"),[37] often come up with reasonable recommendations. These, however, are seldom acted on, but, rather, are subjected to a new panel of researchers. What all the commissions have in common is a desperate attempt to find out something about the "deeper causes" of what-

---

research team, came to the obvious conclusion "that the criminal's lack of concern about being punished is causing a major and immediate crisis." See Tom Wicker, "Crime and the Courts," in the New York *Times*, April 7, 1970.

[37] On April 28, 1970.

ever the problem happens to be—especially if it is the problem of violence—and since "deeper" causes are, by definition, concealed, the final result of such team research is all too often nothing but hypothesis and undemonstrated theory. The net effect is that research has become a substitute for action, and the "deeper causes" are overgrowing the obvious ones, which are frequently so simple that no "serious" and "learned" person could be asked to give them any attention. To be sure, to find remedies for obvious shortcomings does not guarantee solution of the problem; but to neglect them means that the problem will not even be properly defined.[38] Research has become a technique of evasion, and this has surely not helped the already undermined reputation of science.

Since disobedience and defiance of authority are such a general mark of our time, it is tempting to view civil disobedience as a mere special case. From the jurist's viewpoint, the law is violated by the civil, no less than the criminal, disobedient, and it is understandable that people, especially if they happen to be lawyers, should suspect that civil disobedience, precisely because it is exerted in public, is at the root of the criminal variety[39]—all evidence and arguments to the contrary notwithstanding, for evidence

---

[38] There is, for example, the well-known over-researched fact that children in slum schools do not learn. Among the more obvious causes is the fact that many such children arrive at school without having had breakfast and are desperately hungry. There are a number of "deeper" causes for their failure to learn, and it is very uncertain that breakfast would help. What is not at all uncertain is that even a class of geniuses could not be taught if they happened to be hungry.

[39] Justice Charles E. Whittaker, like many others in the profession, "attributes the crisis to ideas of civil disobedience." See Wilson Carey McWilliams, *op. cit.*, p. 211.

73

"to demonstrate that acts of civil disobedience . . . lead to . . . a propensity toward crime" is not "insufficient" but simply nonexistent.[40] Although it is true that radical movements and, certainly, revolutions attract criminal elements, it would be neither correct nor wise to equate the two; criminals are as dangerous to political movements as they are to society as a whole. Moreover, while civil disobedience may be considered an indication of a significant loss of the law's authority (though it can hardly be seen as its cause), criminal disobedience is nothing more than the inevitable consequences of a disastrous erosion of police competence and power. Proposals for probing the "criminal mind," either with Rorschach tests or by intelligence agents, sound sinister, but they, too, belong among the techniques of evasion. An incessant flow of sophisticated hypotheses about the mind—this most elusive of man's properties—of the criminal submerges the solid fact that no one is able to catch his body, just as the hypothetical assumption of policemen's *latent* negative attitudes" covers up their overt negative record in solving crimes.[41]

Civil disobedience arises when a significant number of citizens have become convinced either that the normal channels of change no longer function, and grievances will not be heard or acted upon, or that, on the contrary, the government is about to change and has embarked upon and persists in modes of action whose legality and constitutionality are open to grave doubt. Instances are numerous: seven years of an undeclared war in Vietnam; the growing influence of secret agencies on public affairs; open or thinly veiled threats to liberties guaranteed under the First Amendment; attempts to deprive the Senate of its constitu-

[40] *To Establish Justice . . . , op. cit.*, p. 109.

[41] *Law and Order Reconsidered, op. cit.*, p. 291.

74

tional powers, followed by the President's invasion of Cambodia in open disregard for the Constitution, which explicitly requires congressional approval for the beginning of a war; not to mention the Vice President's even more ominous reference to resisters and dissenters as " 'vultures' . . . and 'parasites' [whom] we can afford to separate . . . from our society with no more regret than we should feel over discarding rotten apples from a barrel"—a reference that challenges not only the laws of the United States, but every legal order.[42] In other words, civil disobedience can be tuned to necessary and desirable change or to necessary and desirable preservation or restoration of the *status quo*—the preservation of rights guaranteed under the First Amendment, or the restoration of the proper balance of power in the government, which is jeopardized by the executive branch as well as by the enormous growth of federal power at the expense of states' rights. In neither case can civil disobedience be equated with criminal disobedience.

There is all the difference in the world between the criminal's avoiding the public eye and the civil disobedient's taking the law into his own hands in open defiance. This distinction between an open violation of the law, performed in public, and a clandestine one is so glaringly obvious that it can be neglected only by prejudice or ill will. It is now recognized by all serious writers on the subject and clearly is the primary condition for all attempts that argue for the compatibility of civil disobedience with law and the American institutions of government. More-

[42] *The New Yorker*'s many excellent comments on the administration's almost open contempt of this country's constitutional and legal order, in its "Talk of the Town" column, are especially recommended.

over, the common lawbreaker, even if he belongs to a criminal organization, acts for his own benefit alone; he refuses to be overpowered by the consent of all others and will yield only to the violence of the law-enforcement agencies. The civil disobedient, though he is usually dissenting from a majority, acts in the name and for the sake of a group; he defies the law and the established authorities on the ground of basic dissent, and not because he as an individual wishes to make an exception for himself and to get away with it. If the group he belongs to is significant in numbers and standing, one is tempted to classify him as a member of one of John C. Calhoun's "concurrent majorities," that is, sections of the population that are unanimous in their dissent. The term, unfortunately, is tainted by proslavery and racist arguments, and in the *Disquisition on Government*, where it occurs, it covers only interests, not opinions and convictions, of minorities that feel threatened by "dominant majorities." The point, at any rate, is that we are dealing here with organized minorities that are too important, not merely in numbers, but in *quality of opinion*, to be safely disregarded. For Calhoun was certainly right when he held that in questions of great national importance the "concurrence or acquiescence of the various portions of the community" are a prerequisite of constitutional government.[43] To think of disobedient minorities as rebels and traitors is against the letter and spirit of a Constitution whose framers were especially sensitive to the dangers of unbridled majority rule.

Of all the means that civil disobedients may use in the course of persuasion and of the dramatization of issues, the only one that can justify their being called "rebels" is the means of violence. Hence, the second generally accepted

---

[43] *A Disquisition on Government* (1853), New York, 1947, p. 67.

necessary characteristic of civil disobedience is nonviolence, and it follows that "civil disobedience is not revolution. . . . The civil disobedient accepts, while the revolutionary rejects, the frame of established authority and the general legitimacy of the system of laws."[44] This second distinction between the revolutionary and the civil disobedient, so plausible at first glance, turns out to be more difficult to sustain than the distinction between civil disobedient and criminal. The civil disobedient shares with the revolutionary the wish "to change the world," and the changes he wishes to accomplish can be drastic indeed—as, for instance, in the case of Gandhi, who is always quoted as the great example, in this context, of nonviolence. (Did Gandhi accept the "frame of established authority," which was British rule of India? Did he respect the "general legitimacy of the system of laws" in the colony?)

"Things of this world are in so constant a flux that nothing remains long in the same state."[45] If this sentence, written by Locke about three hundred years ago, were uttered today, it would sound like the understatement of the century. Still, it may remind us that change is not a modern phenomenon, but is inherent in a world inhabited and established by human beings, who come into it, by birth, as strangers and newcomers (νέοι, the new ones, as the Greeks used to call the young), and depart from it just when they have acquired the experience and familiarity that may in certain rare cases enable them to be "wise" in the ways of the world. "Wise men" have played various and sometimes significant roles in human affairs, but the point is that they have always been old men, about to dis-

[44] Carl Cohen, *op. cit.*, p. 3.

[45] Locke, *The Second Treatise of Government*, No. 157.

appear from the world. Their wisdom, acquired in the proximity of departure, cannot rule a world exposed to the constant onslaught of the inexperience and "foolishness" of newcomers, and it is likely that without this interrelated condition of natality and mortality, which guarantees change and makes the rule of wisdom impossible, the human race would have become extinct long ago out of unbearable boredom.

Change is constant, inherent in the human condition, but the velocity of change is not. It varies greatly from country to country, from century to century. Compared with the coming and going of the generations, the flux of the world's things occurs so slowly that the world offers an almost stable habitat to those who come and stay and go. Or so it was for thousands of years—including the early centuries of the modern age, when first the notion of change for change's sake, under the name of progress, made its appearance. Ours is perhaps the first century in which the speed of change in the things of the world has outstripped the change of its inhabitants. (An alarming symptom of this turnabout is the steadily shrinking span of the generations. From the traditional standard of three or four generations to a century, which corresponded to a "natural" generation gap between fathers and sons, we have now come to the point where four or five years of difference in age are sufficient to establish a gap between the generations.) But even under the extraordinary conditions of the twentieth century, which make Marx's admonition to change the world sound like an exhortation to carry coals to Newcastle, it can hardly be said that man's appetite for change has canceled his need for stability. It is well known that the most radical revolutionary will become a conservative on the day after the revolution. Obviously, neither man's capacity for change nor his capacity for preservation is boundless, the former being limited by the extension of the past into the present—no man begins *ab ovo*—and the latter by the unpredictability of the future. Man's urge for change and his need for stability have always balanced and checked each other, and our current vocabulary, which distinguishes between two factions, the progressives and the conservatives, indicates a state of affairs in which this balance has been thrown out of order.

No civilization—the man-made artifact to house successive generations—would ever have been possible without a framework of stability, to provide the wherein for the flux of change. Foremost among the stabilizing factors, more enduring than customs, manners, and traditions, are the legal systems that regulate our life in the world and our daily affairs with each other. This is the reason it is inevitable that law in a time of rapid change will appear as "a restraining force, thus a negative influence in a world which admires positive action."[46] The variety of such systems is great, both in time and in space, but they all have one thing in common—the thing that justifies us in using the same word for phenomena as different as the Roman *lex*, the Greek νόμς, the Hebrew *torah*—and this is that they were designed to insure stability. (There is another general characteristic of the law: that it is not universally valid, but is either territorially bound or, as in the instance of Jewish law, ethnically restricted; but this does not concern us here. Where both characteristics, stability and limited validity, are absent—where the so-called "laws" of history or nature, for instance, as they are interpreted by the head of state, maintain a "legality" that can change from day to day and that claims validity for all mankind—we are in fact confronted with lawlessness, though not with anarchy, since order can be maintained by means of compulsive organization. The net result, at

[46] Edward H. Levi, *op. cit.*

79

any rate, is criminalization of the whole governmental apparatus, as we know from totalitarian government.)

Because of the unprecedented rate of change in our time and because of the challenge that change poses to the legal order—from the side of the government, as we have seen, as well as from the side of disobedient citizens—it is now widely held that changes can be effected by law, as distinguished from the earlier notion that "legal action [that is, Supreme Court decisions] can influence ways of living."[47] Both opinions seem to me to be based on an error about what the law can achieve and what it cannot. The law can indeed stabilize and legalize change once it has occurred, but the change itself is always the result of extralegal action. To be sure, the Constitution itself offers a quasi-legal way to challenge the law by breaking it, but, quite apart from the question of whether or not such breaches are acts of disobedience, the Supreme Court has the right to choose among the cases brought before it, and this choice is inevitably influenced by public opinion. The bill recently passed in Massachusetts to force a test of the legality of the Vietnam war, which the Supreme Court refused to decide upon, is a case in point. Is it not obvious that this legal action—very significant indeed—was the result of the civil disobedience of draft resisters, and that its aim was to legalize servicemen's refusal of combat duty? The whole body of labor legislation—the right to collective bargaining, the right to organize and to strike—was preceded by decades of frequently violent disobedience of what ultimately proved to be obsolete laws.

The history of the Fourteenth Amendment perhaps offers an especially instructive example of the relation be-

[47] J. D. Hyman, "Segregation and the Fourteenth Amendment," in *Essays in Constitutional Law,* Robert G. McCloskey, ed., New York, 1957, p. 379.

tween law and change. It was meant to translate into constitutional terms the change that had come about as the result of the Civil War. This change was not accepted by the Southern states, with the result that the provisions for racial equality were not enforced for roughly a hundred years. An even more striking example of the inability of the law to enforce change, is, of course, the Eighteenth Amendment, concerning Prohibition, which had to be repealed because it proved to be unenforceable.[48] The Fourteenth Amendment, on the other hand, was finally enforced by the legal action of the Supreme Court, but, although one may argue that it had always been "the plain responsibility of the Supreme Court to cope with state laws that deny racial equality,"[49] the plain fact is that the court chose to do so only when civil-rights movements that, as far as Southern laws were concerned, were clearly movements of civil disobedience had brought about a drastic change in the attitudes of both black and white citizens. Not the law, but civil disobedience brought into the open the "American dilemma" and, perhaps for the first time, forced upon the nation the recognition of the enormity of the crime, not just of slavery, but of chattel slavery—"unique among all such systems known to civilization"[50]—the responsibility for which the people have inherited, together with so many blessings, from their forefathers.

[48] The widespread disobedience of the Prohibition amendment has, however, "no rightful claim to be called disobedience," because it was not practiced in public. See Nicholas W. Puner, *op. cit.*, p. 653.

[49] Robert G. McCloskey in *op. cit.*, p. 352.

[50] On this important point, which explains why emancipation had such disastrous consequences in the United States, see the splendid study *Slavery* by Stanley M. Elkins, New York, 1959.

III

THE PERSPECTIVE of very rapid change suggests that there is "every likelihood of a progressively expanding role for civil disobedience in . . . modern democracies."[51] If "civil disobedience is here to stay," as many have come to believe, the question of its compatibility with the law is of prime importance; the answer to it may well decide whether or not the institutions of liberty will prove flexible enough to survive the onslaught of change without civil war and without revolution. The literature on the subject is inclined to argue the case for civil disobedience on the rather narrow grounds of the First Amendment, admitting its need of being "expanded" and expressing the hope "that future Supreme Court decisions will establish a new theory as to [its] place."[52] But the First Amendment unequivocally defends only "the freedom of speech and of the press," whereas the extent to which "the right of the people peacefully to assemble and to petition the government for a redress of grievances" protects freedom of action is open to interpretation and controversy. According to Supreme Court decisions, "conduct under the First

[51] Christian Bay, *op. cit.*, p. 483.

[52] Harrop A. Freeman, *op. cit.*, p. 23.

Amendment does not enjoy the same latitude as speech does," and "conduct, as opposed to speech, is [of course] endemic" to civil disobedience.[53]

However, what is basically at stake here is not whether, and to what extent, civil disobedience can be justified by the First Amendment, but, rather, with what *concept* of law it is compatible. I shall argue in what follows that although the phenomenon of civil disobedience is today a world-wide phenomenon and even though it has attracted the interest of jurisprudence and political science only recently in the United States, it still is primarily American in origin and substance; that no other country, and no other language, has even a word for it, and that the American republic is the only government having at least a chance to cope with it—not, perhaps, in accordance with the statutes, but in accordance with the *spirit* of its laws. The United States owes its origin to the American Revolution, and this revolution carried within it a new, never fully articulated concept of law, which was the result of no theory but had been formed by the extraordinary experiences of the early colonists. It would be an event of great significance to find a constitutional niche for civil disobedience—of no less significance, perhaps, than the event

[53] Nicholas W. Puner, *op. cit.*, p. 694. For the meaning of the First Amendment's guarantee, see especially Edward S. Corwin, *The Constitution and What It Means Today*, Princeton, 1958. As to the question to what extent freedom of action is protected by the First Amendment, Corwin points out: "Historically, the right of petition is a primary right, the right peaceably to assemble a subordinate and instrumental right. . . . Today, however, the right of peaceable assembly is '. . . cognate to those of free speech and free press and is equally fundamental. . . . The holding of meetings for peaceable political action cannot be proscribed. These who assist in the conduct of such meetings cannot be branded as criminals on that score'" (pp. 203-204).

of the founding of the *constitutio libertatis,* nearly two hundred years ago.

The citizen's moral obligation to obey the laws has traditionally been derived from the assumption that he either consented to them or actually was his own legislator; that under the rule of law men are not subject to an alien will but obey only themselves—with the result, of course, that every person is at the same time his own master and his own slave, and that what is seen as the original conflict between the citizen, concerned with the public good, and the self, pursuing his private happiness, is internalized. This is in essence the Rousseauan-Kantian solution to the problem of obligation, and its defect, from my point of view, is that it turns again on conscience—on the relation between me and myself.[54] From the point of view of modern political science, the trouble lies in the fictitious origin of consent: "Many . . . write as if there were a social contract or some similar basis for political obligation to obey the majority's will," wherefore the argument usually preferred is: We in a democracy have to obey the law because we have the right to vote.[55] But it is precisely these voting rights, universal suffrage in free elections, as a sufficient

---

[54] Another important defect has been pointed out by Hegel: "To be one's own master and servant seems to be better than to be somebody else's servant. However, the relation between freedom and nature, if . . . nature is being oppressed by one's own self, is much more artificial than the relation in natural law, according to which the domineering and commanding part is outside the living individual. In the latter case, the individual as a living entity retains its autonomous identity. . . . It is opposed by an alien power. . . . [Otherwise] its inner harmony is destroyed." In *Differenz des Fichte'schen und Schelling'schen Systems der Philosophie* (1801), Felix Meiner edition, p. 70.

[55] Christian Bay, *op. cit.,* p. 483.

basis for a democracy and for the claim of public freedom, that have come under attack.

Still, the proposition set forth by Eugene Rostow that what needs to be considered is "the citizen's moral obligation to the law *in a society of consent*" seems to me crucial. If Montesquieu was right—and I believe he was—that there is such a thing as "the spirit of the laws," which varies from country to country and is different in the various forms of government, then we may say that consent, not in the very old sense of mere acquiescence, with its distinction between rule over willing subjects and rule over unwilling ones, but in the sense of active support and continuing participation in all matters of public interest, is the spirit of American law. Theoretically, this consent has been construed to be the result of a social contract, which in its more common form—the contract between a people and its government—is indeed easy to denounce as mere fiction. However, the point is that it was no mere fiction in the American prerevolutionary experience, with its numerous covenants and agreements, from the Mayflower Compact to the establishment of the thirteen colonies as an entity. When Locke formulated his social-contract theory, which supposedly explained the aboriginal beginnings of civil society, he indicated in a side remark which model he actually had in mind: "In the beginning, all the world was America."[56]

In theory, the seventeenth century knew and combined under the name of "social contract" three altogether different kinds of such aboriginal agreements. There was, *first,* the example of the Biblical covenant, which was concluded between a people as a whole and its God, by virtue of which the people consented to obey whatever laws an

[56] *Op. cit.,* No. 49.

all-powerful divinity might choose to reveal to it. Had this Puritan version of consent prevailed, it would, as John Cotton rightly remarked, have "set up Theocracy . . . as the best form of government."[57] There was, *second,* the Hobbesian variety, according to which every individual concludes an agreement with the strictly secular authorities to insure his safety, for the protection of which he relinquishes all rights and powers. I shall call this the vertical version of the social contract. It is, of course, inconsistent with the American understanding of government, because it claims for the government a monopoly of power for the benefit of all subjects, who themselves have neither rights nor powers as long as their physical safety is guaranteed; the American republic, in contrast, rests on the power of the people—the old Roman *potestas in populo*—and power granted to the authorities is delegated power, which can be revoked. There was, *third,* Locke's aborginal social contract, which brought about not government but society—the word being understood in the sense of the Latin *societas,* an "alliance" between all individual members, who contract for their government after they have mutually bound themselves. I shall call this the horizontal version of the social contract. This contract limits the power of each individual member but leaves intact the power of society; society then establishes government "upon the plain ground of an original contract among independent individuals."[58]

All contracts, covenants, and agreements rest on mutuality, and the great advantage of the horizontal version of the social contract is that this mutuality binds each mem-

[57] See my discussion of Puritanism and its influence on the American Revolution in *On Revolution,* New York, 1963, pp. 171ff.

[58] John Adams, *Novanglus. Works,* Boston, 1851, vol. IV, p. 110.

ber to his fellow citizens. This is the only form of government in which people are bound together not through historical memories or ethnic homogeneity, as in the nation-state, and not through Hobbes's Leviathan, which "overawes them all" and thus unites them, but through the strength of mutual promises. In Locke's view, this meant that society remains intact even if "the government is dissolved" or breaks its agreement with society, developing into a tyranny. Once established, society, as long as it exists at all, can never be thrown back into the lawlessness and anarchy of the state of nature. In Locke's words, "the power that every individual gave the society, when he entered into it, can never revert to the individuals again, as long as the society lasts, but will always remain in the community."[59] This is indeed a new version of the old *potestas in populo,* for the consequence is that, in contrast to earlier theories of the right to resistance, whereby the people could act only "when their Chains are on," they now had the right, again in Locke's words, "to prevent" the chaining.[60] When the signers of the Declaration of Independence "mutually pledged" their lives, their fortunes, and their sacred honor, they were thinking in this vein of specifically American experiences as well as in terms of the generalization and conceptualization of these experiences by Locke.

Consent—meaning that voluntary membership must be assumed for every citizen in the community—is obviously (except in the case of naturalization) at least as open to the reproach of being a fiction as the aboriginal contract. The argument is correct legally and historically but not existentially and theoretically. Every man is born a

[59] *Op. cit.,* No. 220.

[60] *Ibid.,* No. 243.

member of a particular community and can survive only if he is welcomed and made at home within it. A kind of consent is implied in every newborn's factual situation; namely, a kind of conformity to the rules under which the great game of the world is played in the particular group to which he belongs by birth. We all live and survive by a kind of *tacit consent,* which, however, it would be difficult to call voluntary. How can we will what is there anyhow? We might call it voluntary, though, when the child happens to be born into a community in which dissent is also a legal and *de-facto* possibility once he has grown into a man. Dissent implies consent, and is the hallmark of free government; one who knows that he may dissent knows also that he somehow consents when he does not dissent.

Consent as it is implied in the right to dissent—the spirit of American law and the quintessence of American government—spells out and articulates the tacit consent given in exchange for the community's tacit welcome of new arrivals, of the inner immigration through which it constantly renews itself. Seen in this perspective, tacit consent is not a fiction; it is inherent in the human condition. However, the general tacit consent—the "tacit agreement, a sort of *consensus universalis,*" as Tocqueville called it[61]— must be carefully distinguished from consent to specific laws or specific policies, which it does not cover even if they are the result of majority decisions.[62] It is often ar-

[61] "The republican government exists in America, without contention or opposition, without proofs or arguments, by a tacit agreement, a sort of *consensus universalis.*" *Democracy in America,* New York, 1945, vol. I, p. 419.

[62] For the importance of this distinction, see Hans Morgenthau, *Truth and Power,* 1970, pp. 19 ff.; and *The New Republic,* January 22, 1966, pp. 16-18.

gued that the consent to the Constitution, the *consensus universalis,* implies consent to statutory laws as well, because in representative government the people have helped to make them. This consent, I think, is indeed entirely fictitious; under the present circumstances, at any rate, it has lost all plausibility. Representative government itself is in a crisis today, partly because it has lost, in the course of time, all institutions that permitted the citizens' actual participation, and partly because it is now gravely affected by the disease from which the party system suffers: bureaucratization and the two parties' tendency to represent nobody except the party machines.

At any rate, the current danger of rebellion in the United States arises not from dissent and resistance to particular laws, executive orders, and national policies, not even from denunciation of the "system" or the "establishment" with its familiar overtones of outrage at the low moral standards of those in high places and the protective atmosphere of connivance that surrounds them. What we are confronted with is a constitutional crisis of the first order, and this crisis has been effected by two very different factors whose unfortunate coincidence has resulted in the particular poignancy as well as general confusion of the situation. There are the frequent challenges to the Constitution by the administration, with the consequential loss of confidence in constitutional processes by the people, that is, the withdrawal of consent; and there has come into the open, at about the same time, the more radical unwillingness of certain sections of the population to recognize the *consensus universalis.*

Tocqueville predicted almost a hundred and fifty years ago that "the most formidable of all the ills that threaten the future of the Union arises," not from slavery, whose abolition he foresaw, but "from the presence of a black population upon its territory."[63] And the reason he could predict the future of Negroes and Indians for more than a century ahead lies in the simple and frightening fact that these people had never been included in the original *consensus universalis* of the American republic. There was nothing in the Constitution or in the intent of the framers that could be so construed as to include the slave people in the original compact. Even those who pleaded eventual emancipation thought in terms of segregation of Negroes or, preferably, of deportation. This is true of Jefferson—"Nothing is more certain written in the book of fate than that these people are to be free; nor is it less certain that the two races, equally free, cannot live in the same government"—as it is true of Lincoln, who tried, as late as 1862, "when a deputation of colored men came to see [him] . . . to persuade them to set up a colony in Central America."[64] It was the tragedy of the abolitionist movement, which in its earlier stages had also proposed deportation and colonization (to Liberia), that it could appeal only to individual conscience, and neither to the law of the land nor to the opinion of the country. This may explain its strong general anti-institutional bias, its abstract morality, which condemned all institutions as evil because they tolerated the evil of slavery, and which certainly did not help in promoting those elementary measures of humane reform by which in all other countries the slaves were gradually emancipated into the free society.[65]

We know that this original crime could not be rem-

---

[63] *Op. cit.,* p. 356.

[64] Hofstadter, *op. cit.,* p. 130.

[65] Elkins, in Part IV of his book noted earlier, gives an excellent analysis of the sterility of the abolitionist movement.

edied by the Fourteenth and Fifteenth Amendments; on the contrary, the *tacit* exclusion from the *tacit* consensus was made more conspicuous by the inability or unwillingness of the federal government to enforce its own laws, and as time went by and wave after wave of immigrants came to the country, it was even more obvious that blacks, now free, and born and bred in the country, were the only ones for whom it was not true that, in Bancroft's words, "the welcome of the Commonwealth was as wide as sorrow."[66] We know the result, and we need not be surprised that the present belated attempts to welcome the Negro population explicitly into the otherwise tacit *consensus universalis* of the nation are not trusted. (An explicit constitutional amendment, addressed specifically to the Negro people of America, might have underlined the great change more dramatically for these people who had never been welcome, assuring them of its finality. Supreme Court decisions are constitutional interpretations, of which the Dred Scott decision, which held, in 1857, that "Negroes are not and cannot be citizens in the meaning of the federal Constitution," is one.[67] The failure of Congress to propose such an amendment is striking in the light of the overwhelming vote for a constitutional amendment to

[66] See George Bancroft, *The History of the United States*, abridged edition by Russell B. Nye, Chicago, 1966, p. 44.

[67] The case of *Dred Scott* v. *Sandford* came on appeal before the Supreme Court. Scott, a slave from Missouri, had been taken by his owner to Illinois and other territory where slavery was outlawed. Back in Missouri, Scott sued his owner, "arguing that these journeys to free areas had made him a free man." The court decided that Scott could "not bring suit in federal courts . . . because Negroes are not and cannot be citizens in the meaning of the federal Constitution." See Robert McCloskey, *The American Supreme Court*, Chicago, 1966, pp. 93-95.

cure the infinitely milder discriminatory practices against women.) At any rate, attempts of integration often are met by rebuffs from black organizations, while quite a number of their leaders care little about the rules of nonviolence for civil disobedience and, often, just as little about the issues at stake—the Vietnam war, specific defects in our institutions—because they are in open rebellion against all of them. And although they have been able to attract to their cause the extreme fringe of radical disobedience, which without them would probably have withered away long ago, their instinct tells them to disengage themselves even from these supporters, who, their rebellious spirit notwithstanding, were included in the original contract out of which rose the tacit *consensus universalis.*

Consent, in the American understanding of the term, relies on the horizontal version of the social contract, and not on majority decisions. (On the contrary, much of the thinking of the framers of the Constitution concerned safeguards for dissenting minorities.) The moral content of this consent is like the moral content of all agreements and contracts; it consists in the obligation to keep them. This obligation is inherent in all promises. Every organization of men, be it social or political, ultimately relies on man's capacity for making promises and keeping them. The only strictly moral duty of the citizen is this twofold willingness to give and keep reliable assurance as to his future conduct, which forms the prepolitical condition of all other, specifically political, virtues. Thoreau's often quoted statement "The only obligation which I have a right to assume is to do at any time what I think right" might well be varied to: The only obligation which I *as a citizen* have a right to assume is to make and to keep promises.

Promises are the uniquely human way of ordering the future, making it predictable and reliable to the extent that this is humanly possible. And since the predictability of the future can never be absolute, promises are qualified by two essential limitations. We are bound to keep our promises provided that no unexpected circumstances arise, and provided that the mutuality inherent in all promises is not broken. There exist a great number of circumstances that may cause a promise to be broken, the most important one in our context being the general circumstance of change. And violation of the inherent mutuality of promises can also be caused by many factors, the only relevant one in our context being the failure of the established authorities to keep to the original conditions. Examples of such failures have become only too numerous; there is the case of an "illegal and immoral war," the case of an increasingly impatient claim to power by the executive branch of government, the case of chronic deception, coupled with deliberate attacks on the freedoms guaranteed under the First Amendment, whose chief political function has always been to make *chronic* deception impossible; and there has been, last but not least, the case of violations (in the form of war-oriented or other government-directed research) of the specific trust of the universities that gave them protection against political interference and social pressure. As to the debates about the last, those who attack these misuses and those who defend them unfortunately incline to agree on the basically wrong premise that the universities are mere "mirrors for the larger society," an argument best answered by Edward H. Levi, the president of the University of Chicago: "It is sometimes said that society will achieve the kind of education it deserves. Heaven help us if this is so."[68]

[68] *Point of View. Talks on Education,* Chicago, 1969, pp. 139 and 170.

"The spirit of the laws," as Montesquieu understood it, is the principle by which people living under a particular legal system act and are inspired to act. Consent, the spirit of American laws, is based on the notion of a mutually binding contract, which established first the individual colonies and then the union. A contract presupposes a plurality of at least two, and every association established and acting according to the principle of consent, based on mutual promise, presupposes a plurality that does not dissolve but is shaped into the form of a union—*e pluribus unum*. If the individual members of the community thus formed should choose not to retain a restricted autonomy, if they should choose to disappear into complete unity, such as the *union sacrée* of the French nation, all talk about the citizen's *moral* relation to the law would be mere rhetoric.

Consent and the right to dissent became the inspiring and organizing principles of action that taught the inhabitants of this continent the "art of associating together," from which sprang those voluntary associations whose role Tocqueville was the first to notice, with amazement, admiration, and some misgiving; he thought them the peculiar strength of the American political system.[69] The few chapters he devoted to them are still by far the best in the not very large literature on the subject. The words with which he introduced it—"In no country in the world has the principle of association been more successfully used or applied to a greater multitude of objects than in America"—are no less true today than they were nearly a hundred and fifty years ago; and neither is the conclu-

---

[69] All the following citations of Tocqueville are from *op. cit.*, vol. I, chap. 12, and vol. II, book ii, chap. 5.

sion that "nothing . . . is more deserving of our attention than the moral and intellectual associations of America." Voluntary associations are not parties; they are *ad-hoc* organizations that pursue short-term goals and disappear when the goal has been reached. Only in the case of their prolonged failure and of an aim of great importance may they "constitute, as it were, a separate nation in the midst of the nation, a government within the government." (This happened in 1861, about thirty years after Tocqueville wrote these words, and it could happen again; the challenge of the Massachusetts legislature to the foreign policy of the administration is a clear warning.) Alas, under the conditions of mass society, especially in the big cities, it is no longer true that their spirit "pervades every act of social life," and while this may have resulted in a certain decline in the huge number of joiners in the population—of Babbitts, who are the specifically American version of the Philistine—the perhaps welcome refusal to form associations "for the smallest undertakings" is paid for by an evident decline in the appetite for action. For Americans still regard association as "the only means they have for acting," and rightly so. The last few years, with the mass demonstrations in Washington, often organized on the spur of the moment, have shown to what an unexpected extent the old traditions are still alive. Tocqueville's account could almost be written today: "As soon as several of the inhabitants of the United States have taken up an opinion or a feeling which they wish to promote in the world," or have found some fault they wish to correct, "they look out for mutual assistance, and as soon as they have found one another out, they combine. *From that moment, they are no longer isolated men but a power seen from afar,* whose actions serve for an example and whose language is listened to" (my italics).

It is my contention that civil disobedients are nothing but the latest form of voluntary association, and that they are thus quite in tune with the oldest traditions of the country. What could better describe them than Tocqueville's words "The citizens who form the minority associate in order, first, to show their numerical strength and so to diminish the moral power of the majority"? To be sure, it has been a long time since "moral and intellectual associations" could be found among voluntary associations—which, on the contrary, seem to have been formed only for the protection of special interests, of pressure groups and the lobbyists who represented them in Washington. I do not doubt that the dubious reputation of the lobbyists is deserved, just as the dubious reputation of the politicians in this country has frequently been amply deserved. However, the fact is that the pressure groups are also voluntary associations, and that they are recognized in Washington, where their influence is sufficiently great for them to be called an "assistant government";[70] indeed, the number of registered lobbyists exceeds by far the number of congressmen.[71] This public recognition is no small matter, for such "assistance" was no more foreseen in the Constitution and its First Amendment than freedom of association as a form of political action.[72]

[70] See Carl Joachim Friedrich, *Constitutional Government and Democracy*, Boston, 1950, p. 464.

[71] Edward S. Corwin, *loc. cit.*

[72] I do not doubt that "civil disobedience is a proper procedure to bring a law, believed to be unjust or invalid, into court or before the bar of public opinion." The question is only " . . . if this is indeed one of the rights recognized by the First Amendment," in the words of Harrop A. Freeman, *op. cit.*, p. 25.

No doubt "the danger of civil disobedience is elemental,"[73] but it is not different from, nor is it greater than, the dangers inherent in the right to free association, and of these Tocqueville, his admiration notwithstanding, was not unaware. (John Stuart Mill, in his review of the first volume of *Democracy in America,* formulated the gist of Tocqueville's apprehension: "The capacity of coöperation for a common purpose, heretofore a monopolized instrument of power in the hands of the higher classes, is now a most formidable one in those of the lowest.")[74] Tocqueville knew that "the tyrannical control that these societies exercise is often far more insupportable than the authority possessed over society by the government which they attack." But he knew also that "the liberty of association has become a necessary guarantee against the tyranny of the majority," that "a dangerous expedient is used to obviate a still more formidable danger," and, finally, that "it is by the enjoyment of dangerous freedom that the Americans learn the art of rendering the dangers of freedom less formidable." In any event, "if men are to remain civilized or to become so, the art of associating together must grow and improve *in the same ratio in which the equality of conditions is increased*" (my italics).

We need not go into the old debates about the glories and the dangers of equality, the good and the evil of democracy, to understand that all evil demons could be let loose if the original contractual model of the associations—mutual promises with the moral imperative *pacta sunt servanda*—should be lost. Under today's circumstances, this could happen if these groups, like their counterparts in

[73] Nicholas W. Puner, *op. cit.,* p. 707.

[74] Reprinted as Introduction to the Schocken Paperback edition of Tocqueville, 1961.

other countries, were to substitute ideological commitments, political or other, for actual goals. When an association is no longer capable or willing to unite "into one channel the efforts of *divergent* minds" (Tocqueville), it has lost its gift for action. What threatens the student movement, the chief civil-disobedience group of the moment, is not just vandalism, violence, bad temper, and worse manners, but the growing infection of the movement with ideologies (Maoism, Castroism, Stalinism, Marxism-Leninism, and the like), which in fact split and dissolve the association.

Civil disobedience and voluntary association are phenomena practically unknown anywhere else. (The political terminology that surrounds them yields only with great difficulty to translation.) It has often been said that the genius of the English people is to muddle through and that the genius of the American people is to disregard theoretical considerations in favor of pragmatic experience and practical action. This is doubtful; undeniable, however, is that the phenomenon of voluntary association has been neglected and that the notion of civil disobedience has only recently received the attention it deserves. In contrast to the conscientious objector, the civil disobedient is a member of a group, and this group, whether we like it or not, is formed in accordance with the same spirit that has informed voluntary associations. The greatest fallacy in the present debate seems to me the assumption that we are dealing with individuals, who pit themselves subjectively and conscientiously against the laws and customs of the community—an assumption that is shared by the defenders and the detractors of civil disobedience. The fact is that we are dealing with organized minorities, who stand against assumed inarticulate, though hardly "silent," majorities, and I think it is undeniable that these majorities

98

have changed in mood and opinion to an astounding degree under the pressure of the minorities. In this respect, it has perhaps been unfortunate that our recent debates have been dominated largely by jurists—lawyers, judges, and other men of law—for they must find it particularly difficult to recognize the civil disobedient as a member of a group rather than to see him as an individual lawbreaker, and hence a potential defendant in court. It is, indeed, the grandeur of court procedure that it is concerned with meting out justice to an individual, and remains unconcerned with everything else—with the *Zeitgeist* or with opinions that the defendant may share with others and try to present in court. The only noncriminal lawbreaker the court recognizes is the conscientious objector, and the only group adherence it is aware of is called "conspiracy"—an utterly misleading charge in such cases, since conspiracy requires not only "breathing together" but secrecy, and civil disobedience occurs in public.

Although civil disobedience is compatible with the *spirit* of American laws, the difficulties of incorporating it into the American legal system and justifying it on purely legal grounds seem to be prohibitive. But these difficulties follow from the nature of the law in general, not from the special spirit of the American legal system. Obviously, "the law cannot justify the violation of the law," even if this violation aims at preventing the violation of another law.[75] It is an altogether different question whether it would not be possible to find a recognized niche for civil disobedience in our institutions of government. This political approach to the problem is strongly suggested by the Supreme Court's recent denial of certiorari to cases in which the government's "illegal and unconstitutional" acts

[75] Carl Cohen, *op. cit.,* p. 7.

with respect to the war in Vietnam were contested, because the court found that these cases involve the so-called "political question doctrine," according to which certain acts of the two other branches of government, the legislative and the executive, "are not reviewable in the courts. The precise status and nature of the doctrine are much in dispute," and the whole doctrine has been called "a smoldering volcano which may now be about to fulfill its long promise of erupting into flaming controversy,"[76] but there is little doubt about the nature of those acts on which the court will not rule and which therefore are left outside legal controls. These acts are characterized by their "momentousness"[77] and by "an unusual need for unquestioning adherence to a political decision already made."[78] Graham Hughes, to whose excellent examination of the political question doctrine I am greatly indebted, immediately adds that "these considerations . . . certainly seem to imply *inter arma silent leges* and cast doubt on the aphorism that it is a Constitution that is being expounded." In other words, the political doctrine is in fact that loophole through which the sovereignty principle and the reason of state doctrine are permitted to filter back, as it were, into a system of government which in principle denies them.[79] Whatever the theory, the facts of the matter suggest that precisely in crucial issues the Supreme Court

[76] Graham Hughes, *op. cit.*, p. 7.

[77] Alexander M. Bickle, as quoted by Hughes, *op. cit.*, p. 10.

[78] Court decision in the case of *Baker* v. *Carr,* as quoted by Hughes, *ibid.,* p. 11.

[79] To quote Justice James Wilson's early remark (in 1793): "To the Constitution of the United States the term sovereignty is totally unknown."

has no more power than an international court: both are unable to enforce decisions that would hurt decisively the interests of sovereign states and both know that their authority depends on prudence, that is, on not raising issues or making decisions that cannot be enforced.

The establishment of civil disobedience among our political institutions might be the best possible remedy for this ultimate failure of judicial review. The first step would be to obtain the same recognition for the civil-disobedient minorities that is accorded the numerous special-interest groups (minority groups, by definition) in the country, and to deal with civil-disobedient groups in the same way as with pressure groups, which, through their representatives —that is, registered lobbyists—are permitted to influence and "assist" Congress by means of persuasion, qualified opinion, and the numbers of their constituents. These minorities of opinion would thus be able to establish themselves as a power that is not only "seen from afar" during demonstrations and other dramatizations of their viewpoint, but is always present and to be reckoned with in the daily business of government. The next step would be to admit publicly that the First Amendment neither in language nor in spirit covers the right of association as it is actually practiced in this country—this precious privilege whose exercise has in fact been (as Tocqueville noted) "incorporated with the manners and customs of the people" for centuries. If there is anything that urgently requires a new constitutional amendment and is worth all the trouble that goes with it, it is certainly this.

Perhaps an emergency was needed before we could find a home for civil disobedience, not only in our political language, but in our political system as well. An emergency is certainly at hand when the established institutions of a country fail to function properly and its authority loses its power, and it is such an emergency in the United States today that has changed voluntary association into civil disobedience and transformed dissent into resistance. It is common knowledge that this condition of latent or overt emergency prevails at present—and, indeed, has prevailed for some time—in large parts of the world; what is new is that this country is no longer an exception. Whether our form of government will survive this century is uncertain, but it is also uncertain that it will not. Wilson Carey McWilliams has wisely said, "When institutions fail, political society depends on men, and men are feeble reeds, prone to acquiesce in—if not to commit—iniquity."[80] Ever since the Mayflower Compact was drafted and signed under a different kind of emergency, voluntary associations have been the specifically American remedy for the failure of institutions, the unreliability of men, and the uncertain nature of the future. As distinguished from other countries, this republic, despite the great turmoil of change and of failure through which it is going at present, may still be in possession of its traditional instruments for facing the future with some measure of confidence.

[80] *Op. cit.,* p. 226.

On Violence

I

THESE REFLECTIONS were provoked by the events and debates of the last few years as seen against the background of the twentieth century, which has become indeed, as Lenin predicted, a century of wars and revolutions, hence a century of that violence which is currently believed to be their common denominator. There is, however, another factor in the present situation which, though predicted by nobody, is of at least equal importance. The technical development of the implements of violence has now reached the point where no political goal could conceivably correspond to their destructive potential or justify their actual use in armed conflict. Hence, warfare—from time immemorial the final merciless arbiter in international disputes—has lost much of its effectiveness and nearly all its glamour. The "apocalyptic" chess game between the superpowers, that is, between those that move on the highest plane of our civilization, is being played according to the rule "if either 'wins' it is the end of both"; [1] it is a game that bears no resemblance to whatever war games preceded it. Its "rational" goal is deterrence, not victory, and the arms

[1] Harvey Wheeler, "The Strategic Calculators," in Nigel Calder, *Unless Peace Comes,* New York, 1968, p. 109.

105

race, no longer a preparation for war, can now be justified only on the grounds that more and more deterrence is the best guarantee of peace. To the question how shall we ever be able to extricate ourselves from the obvious insanity of this position, there is no answer.

Since violence—as distinct from power, force, or strength —always needs *implements* (as Engels pointed out long ago),[2] the revolution of technology, a revolution in toolmaking, was especially marked in warfare. The very substance of violent action is ruled by the means-end category, whose chief characteristic, if applied to human affairs, has always been that the end is in danger of being overwhelmed by the means which it justifies and which are needed to reach it. Since the end of human action, as distinct from the end products of fabrication, can never be reliably predicted, the means used to achieve political goals are more often than not of greater relevance to the future world than the intended goals.

Moreover, while the results of men's actions are beyond the actors' control, violence harbors within itself an additional element of arbitrariness; nowhere does Fortuna, good or ill luck, play a more fateful role in human affairs than on the battlefield, and this intrusion of the utterly unexpected does not disappear when people call it a "random event" and find it scientifically suspect; nor can it be eliminated by simulations, scenarios, game theories, and the like. There is no certainty in these matters, not even an ultimate certainty of mutual destruction under certain calculated circumstances. The very fact that those engaged in the perfection of the means of destruction have finally reached a level of technical development where their aim, namely, warfare, is on the point of dis-

---

[2] *Herrn Eugen Dührings Umwälzung der Wissenschaft* (1878), Part II, ch. 3.

appearing altogether by virtue of the means at its disposal [3] is like an ironical reminder of this all-pervading unpredictability, which we encounter the moment we approach the realm of violence. The chief reason warfare is still with us is neither a secret death wish of the human species, nor an irrepressible instinct of aggression, nor, finally and more plausibly, the serious economic and social dangers inherent in disarmament,[4] but the simple fact that no substitute for this final arbiter in international affairs has yet appeared on the political scene. Was not Hobbes right when he said: "Covenants, without the sword, are but words"?

Nor is a substitute likely to appear so long as national independence, namely, freedom from foreign rule, and the sovereignty of the state, namely, the claim to unchecked and unlimited power in foreign affairs, are identified. (The United States of America is among the few countries where a proper separation of freedom and sovereignty is at least theoretically possible insofar as the very

[3] As General André Beaufre, in "Battlefields of the 1980s," points out: Only "in those parts of the world not covered by nuclear deterrence" is war still possible, and even this "conventional warfare," despite its horrors, is actually already limited by the ever-present threat of escalation into nuclear war. (In Calder, *op. cit.,* p. 3.)

[4] *Report from Iron Mountain,* New York, 1967, the satire on the Rand Corporation's and other think tanks' way of thinking, is probably closer to reality, with its "timid glance over the brink of peace," than most "serious" studies. Its chief argument, that war is so essential to the functioning of our society that we dare not abolish it unless we discover even more murderous ways of dealing with our problems, will shock only those who have forgotten to what an extent the unemployment crisis of the Great Depression was solved only through the outbreak of World War II, or those who conveniently neglect or argue away the extent of present latent unemployment behind various forms of featherbedding.

foundations of the American republic would not be threatened by it. Foreign treaties, according to the Constitution, are part and parcel of the law of the land, and—as Justice James Wilson remarked in 1793—"to the Constitution of the United States the term sovereignty is totally unknown." But the times of such clearheaded and proud separation from the traditional language and conceptual political frame of the European nation-state are long past; the heritage of the American Revolution is forgotten, and the American government, for better and for worse, has entered into the heritage of Europe as though it were its patrimony—unaware, alas, of the fact that Europe's declining power was preceded and accompanied by political bankruptcy, the bankruptcy of the nation-state and its concept of sovereignty.) That war is still the *ultima ratio*, the old continuation of politics by means of violence, in the foreign affairs of the underdeveloped countries is no argument against its obsoleteness, and the fact that only small countries without nuclear and biological weapons can still afford it is no consolation. It is a secret from nobody that the famous random event is most likely to arise from those parts of the world where the old adage "There is no alternative to victory" retains a high degree of plausibility.

Under these circumstances, there are, indeed, few things that are more frightening than the steadily increasing prestige of scientifically minded brain trusters in the councils of government during the last decades. The trouble is not that they are cold-blooded enough to "think the unthinkable," but that they do not *think*. Instead of indulging in such an old-fashioned, uncomputerizable activity, they reckon with the consequences of certain hypothetically assumed constellations without, however, being able to test their hypotheses against actual occurrences. The logical flaw in these hypothetical constructions of future events is always the same: what first appears as a hypothesis—with or without its implied alternatives, according to the level of sophistication—turns immediately, usually after a few paragraphs, into a "fact," which then gives birth to a whole string of similar non-facts, with the result that the purely speculative character of the whole enterprise is forgotten. Needless to say, this is not science but pseudo-science, "the desperate attempt of the social and behavioral sciences," in the words of Noam Chomsky, "to imitate the surface features of sciences that really have significant intellectual content." And the most obvious and "most profound objection to this kind of strategic theory is not its limited usefulness but its danger, for it can lead us to believe we have an understanding of events and control over their flow which we do not have," as Richard N. Goodwin recently pointed out in a review article that had the rare virtue of detecting the "unconscious humor" characteristic of many of these pompous pseudo-scientific theories.[5]

Events, by definition, are occurrences that interrupt routine processes and routine procedures; only in a world in which nothing of importance ever happens could the futurologists' dream come true. Predictions of the future are never anything but projections of present automatic processes and procedures, that is, of occurrences that are likely to come to pass if men do not act and if nothing unexpected happens; every action, for better or worse, and every accident necessarily destroys the whole pattern in whose frame the prediction moves and where it finds its evidence. (Proudhon's passing remark, "The fecundity of the unexpected far exceeds the statesman's prudence," is

[5] Noam Chomsky in *American Power and the New Mandarins*, New York, 1969; Richard N. Goodwin's review of Thomas C. Schelling's *Arms and Influence*, Yale, 1966, in *The New Yorker*, February 17, 1968.

fortunately still true. It exceeds even more obviously the expert's calculations.) To call such unexpected, unpredicted, and unpredictable happenings "random events" or "the last gasps of the past," condemning them to irrelevance or the famous "dustbin of history," is the oldest trick in the trade; the trick, no doubt, helps in clearing up the theory, but at the price of removing it further and further from reality. The danger is that these theories are not only plausible, because they take their evidence from actually discernible present trends, but that, because of their inner consistency, they have a hypnotic effect; they put to sleep our common sense, which is nothing else but our mental organ for perceiving, understanding, and dealing with reality and factuality.

No one engaged in thought about history and politics can remain unaware of the enormous role violence has always played in human affairs, and it is at first glance rather surprising that violence has been singled out so seldom for special consideration.[6] (In the last edition of the Encyclopedia of the Social Sciences "violence" does not even rate an entry.) This shows to what an extent violence and its arbitrariness were taken for granted and therefore neglected; no one questions or examines what is obvious to all. Those who saw nothing but violence in human affairs, convinced that they were "always haphazard, not serious, not precise" (Renan) or that God was forever with the bigger battalions, had nothing more to say about either violence or history. Anybody looking for some kind of sense in the records of the past was almost bound to see violence as a marginal phenomenon. Whether it is Clausewitz calling war "the continuation of politics by other

---

[6] There exists, of course, a large literature on war and warfare, but it deals with the implements of violence, not with violence as such.

means," or Engels defining violence as the accelerator of economic development,[7] the emphasis is on political or economic continuity, on the continuity of a process that remains determined by what preceded violent action. Hence, students of international relations have held until recently that "it was a maxim that a military resolution in discord with the deeper cultural sources of national power could not be stable," or that, in Engels' words, "wherever the power structure of a country contradicts its economic development" it is political power with its means of violence that will suffer defeat.[8]

Today all these old verities about the relation between war and politics or about violence and power have become inapplicable. The Second World War was not followed by peace but by a cold war and the establishment of the military-industrial-labor complex. To speak of "the priority of war-making potential as the principal structuring force in society," to maintain that "economic systems, political philosophies, and corpora juris serve and extend the war system, not vice versa," to conclude that "war itself is the basic social system, within which other secondary modes of social organization conflict or conspire"—all this sounds much more plausible than Engels' or Clausewitz's nineteenth-century formulas. Even more conclusive than this simple reversal proposed by the anonymous author of the *Report from Iron Mountain*—instead of war being "an extension of diplomacy (or of politics, or of the pursuit of economic objectives)," peace is the continuation of war by other means—is the actual development in the techniques of warfare. In the words of the Russian physicist Sakharov, "A thermonuclear war cannot be considered a continuation of politics by other means (according to the

[7] See Engels, *op. cit.*, Part II, ch. 4.

[8] Wheeler, *op. cit.*, p. 107; Engels, *ibidem*.

formula of Clausewitz). It would be a means of universal suicide." [9]

Moreover, we know that "a few weapons could wipe out all other sources of national power in a few moments," [10] that biological weapons have been devised which would enable "small groups of individuals . . . to upset the strategic balance" and would be cheap enough to be produced by "nations unable to develop nuclear striking forces," [11] that "within a very few years" robot soldiers will have made "human soldiers completely obsolete," [12] and that, finally, in conventional warfare the poor countries are much less vulnerable than the great powers precisely because they are "underdeveloped," and because technical superiority can "be much more of a liability than an asset" in guerrilla wars.[13] What all these uncomfortable novelties add up to is a complete reversal in the relationship between power and violence, foreshadowing another reversal in the future relationship between small and great powers. The amount of violence at the disposal of any given country may soon not be a reliable indication of the country's strength or a reliable guarantee against destruction by a substantially smaller and weaker power. And this bears an ominous similarity to one of political science's oldest insights, namely that power cannot be measured in terms of wealth, that an abundance of wealth may erode power, that riches are particularly dangerous to the power

[9] Andrei D. Sakharov, *Progress, Coexistence, and Intellectual Freedom*, New York, 1968, p. 36.

[10] Wheeler, *ibidem*.

[11] Nigel Calder, "The New Weapons," in *op. cit.*, p. 239.

[12] M. W. Thring, "Robots on the March," in Calder, *op. cit.*, p. 169.

[13] Vladimir Dedijer, "The Poor Man's Power," in Calder, *op. cit.*, p. 29.

and well-being of republics—an insight that does not lose in validity because it has been forgotten, especially at a time when its truth has acquired a new dimension of validity by becoming applicable to the arsenal of violence as well.

The more dubious and uncertain an instrument violence has become in international relations, the more it has gained in reputation and appeal in domestic affairs, specifically in the matter of revolution. The strong Marxist rhetoric of the New Left coincides with the steady growth of the entirely non-Marxian conviction, proclaimed by Mao Tse-tung, that "Power grows out of the barrel of a gun." To be sure, Marx was aware of the role of violence in history, but this role was to him secondary; not violence but the contradictions inherent in the old society brought about its end. The emergence of a new society was preceded, but not caused, by violent outbreaks, which he likened to the labor pangs that precede, but of course do not cause, the event of organic birth. In the same vein he regarded the state as an instrument of violence in the command of the ruling class; but the actual power of the ruling class did not consist of or rely on violence. It was defined by the role the ruling class played in society, or, more exactly, by its role in the process of production. It has often been noticed, and sometimes deplored, that the revolutionary Left under the influence of Marx's teachings ruled out the use of violent means; the "dictatorship of the proletariat"—openly repressive in Marx's writings—came after the revolution and was meant, like the Roman dictatorship, to last a strictly limited period. Political assassination, except for a few acts of individual terror perpetrated by small groups of anarchists, was mostly the prerogative of the Right, while organized armed uprisings remained the specialty of the military. The Left remained convinced "that all conspiracies are not only useless but harmful.

They [knew] only too well that revolutions are not made intentionally and arbitrarily, but that they were always and everywhere the necessary result of circumstances entirely independent of the will and guidance of particular parties and whole classes." [14]

On the level of theory there were a few exceptions. Georges Sorel, who at the beginning of the century tried to combine Marxism with Bergson's philosophy of life—the result, though on a much lower level of sophistication, is oddly similar to Sartre's current amalgamation of existentialism and Marxism—thought of class struggle in military terms; yet he ended by proposing nothing more violent than the famous myth of the general strike, a form of action which we today would think of as belonging rather to the arsenal of nonviolent politics. Fifty years ago even this modest proposal earned him the reputation of being a fascist, notwithstanding his enthusiastic approval of Lenin and the Russian Revolution. Sartre, who in his preface to Fanon's *The Wretched of the Earth* goes much farther in his glorification of violence than Sorel in his famous *Reflections on Violence*—farther than Fanon himself, whose argument he wishes to bring to its conclusion—still mentions "Sorel's fascist utterances." This shows to what extent Sartre is unaware of his basic disagreement with Marx on the question of violence, especially when he states that "irrepressible violence . . . is man recreating himself," that it is through "mad fury" that "the wretched of the earth" can "become men." These notions are all the more remarkable because the idea of man creating himself is strictly in the tradition of Hegelian and Marxian thinking; it is the very basis of all leftist humanism. But according to Hegel man "produces" himself through

[14] I owe this early remark of Engels, in a manuscript of 1847, to Jacob Barion, *Hegel und die marxistische Staatslehre*, Bonn, 1963.

thought,[15] whereas for Marx, who turned Hegel's "ideal-ism" upside down, it was labor, the human form of metabolism with nature, that fulfilled this function. And though one may argue that all notions of man creating himself have in common a rebellion against the very factuality of the human condition—nothing is more obvious than that man, whether as member of the species or as an individual, does *not* owe his existence to himself—and that therefore what Sartre, Marx, and Hegel have in common is more relevant than the particular activities through which this non-fact should presumably have come about, still it cannot be denied that a gulf separates the essentially peaceful activities of thinking and laboring from all deeds of violence. "To shoot down a European is to kill two birds with one stone . . . there remain a dead man and a free man," says Sartre in his preface. This is a sentence Marx could never have written.[16]

I quoted Sartre in order to show that this new shift toward violence in the thinking of revolutionaries can remain unnoticed even by one of their most representative and articulate spokesmen,[17] and it is all the more noteworthy for evidently not being an abstract notion in the history of ideas. (If one turns the "idealistic" *concept* of thought upside down, one might arrive at the "materialistic" *concept* of labor; one will never arrive at the notion of violence.) No doubt all this has a logic of its own, but it is one springing from experience, and this experience was utterly unknown to any generation before.

The pathos and the *élan* of the New Left, their credi-

[15] It is quite suggestive that Hegel speaks in this context of "*Sichselbstproduzieren.*" See *Vorlesungen über die Geschichte der Philosophie,* ed. Hoffmeister, p. 114, Leipzig, 1938.

[16] See appendix I, p. 185.

[17] See appendix II, p. 185.

bility, as it were, are closely connected with the weird suicidal development of modern weapons; this is the first generation to grow up under the shadow of the atom bomb. They inherited from their parents' generation the experience of a massive intrusion of criminal violence into politics: they learned in high school and in college about concentration and extermination camps, about genocide and torture,[18] about the wholesale slaughter of civilians in war without which modern military operations are no longer possible even if restricted to "conventional" weapons. Their first reaction was a revulsion against every form of violence, an almost matter-of-course espousal of a politics of nonviolence. The very great successes of this movement, especially in the field of civil rights, were followed by the resistance movement against the war in Vietnam, which has remained an important factor in determining the climate of opinion in this country. But it is no secret that things have changed since then, that the adherents of nonviolence are on the defensive, and it would be futile to say that only the "extremists" are yielding to a glorification of violence and have discovered—like Fanon's Algerian peasants—that "only violence pays." [19]

[18] Noam Chomsky rightly notices among the motives for open rebellion the refusal "to take one's place alongside the 'good German' we have all learned to despise." *Op. cit.*, p. 368.

[19] Frantz Fanon, *The Wretched of the Earth* (1961), Grove Press edition, 1968, p. 61. I am using this work because of its great influence on the present student generation. Fanon himself, however, is much more doubtful about violence than his admirers. It seems that only the book's first chapter, "Concerning Violence," has been widely read. Fanon knows of the "unmixed and total brutality [which], if not immediately combatted, invariably leads to the defeat of the movement within a few weeks" (p. 147).

For the recent escalation of violence in the student movement, see the instructive series "Gewalt" in the German news magazine

The new militants have been denounced as anarchists, nihilists, red fascists, Nazis, and, with considerably more justification, "Luddite machine smashers," [20] and the students have countered with the equally meaningless slogans of "police state" or "latent fascism of late capitalism," and, with considerably more justification, "consumer society." [21] Their behavior has been blamed on all kinds of social and psychological factors—on too much permissiveness in their upbringing in America and on an explosive reaction to too much authority in Germany and Japan, on the lack of freedom in Eastern Europe and too much freedom in the West, on the disastrous lack of jobs for sociology students in France and the superabundance of careers in nearly all fields in the United States—all of which appear locally plausible enough but are clearly contradicted by the fact that the student rebellion is a global phenomenon. A social common denominator of the movement seems out of the question, but it is true that psychologically this generation seems everywhere char-

---

Der Spiegel (February 10, 1969 ff.), and the series "Mit dem Latein am Ende" (Nos. 26 and 27, 1969).

[20] See appendix III, p. 187.

[21] The last of these epithets would make sense if it were meant descriptively. Behind it, however, stands the illusion of Marx's society of free producers, the liberation of the productive forces of society, which in fact has been accomplished not by the revolution but by science and technology. This liberation, furthermore, is not accelerated, but seriously retarded, in all countries that have gone through a revolution. In other words, behind their denunciation of consumption stands the idealization of production, and with it the old idolization of productivity and creativity. "The joy of destruction is a creative joy"—yes indeed, if one believes that "the joy of labor" is productive; destruction is about the only "labor" left that can be done by simple implements without the help of machines, although machines do the job, of course, much more efficiently

acterized by sheer courage, an astounding will to action, and by a no less astounding confidence in the possibility of change.[22] But these qualities are not causes, and if one asks what has actually brought about this wholly unexpected development in universities all over the world, it seems absurd to ignore the most obvious and perhaps the most potent factor, for which, moreover, no precedent and no analogy exist—the simple fact that technological "progress" is leading in so many instances straight into disaster;[23] that the sciences, taught and learned by this generation, seem not merely unable to undo the disastrous consequences of their own technology but have reached a stage in their development where "there's no damn thing you can do that can't be turned into war."[24] (To be sure, nothing is more important to the integrity of the universities—which, in Senator Fulbright's words, have betrayed a public trust when they became dependent on gov-

---

[22] This appetite for action is especially noticeable in small and relatively harmless enterprises. Students struck successfully against campus authorities who were paying employees in the cafeteria and in buildings and grounds less than the legal minimum. The decision of the Berkeley students to join the fight for transforming an empty university-owned lot into a "People's Park" should be counted among these enterprises, even though it provoked the worst reaction so far from the authorities. To judge from the Berkeley incident, it seems that precisely such "nonpolitical" actions unify the student body behind a radical vanguard. "A student referendum, which saw the heaviest turnout in the history of student voting, found 85 percent of the nearly 15,000 who voted favoring the use of the lot" as a people's park. See the excellent report by Sheldon Wolin and John Schaar, "Berkeley: The Battle of People's Park," *New York Review of Books,* June 19, 1969.

[23] See appendix IV, p. 188.

[24] Thus Jerome Lettvin, of M.I.T., in the New York *Times Magazine,* May 18, 1969.

ernment-sponsored research projects [25]—than a rigorously enforced divorce from war-oriented research and all connected enterprises; but it would be naïve to expect this to change the nature of modern science or hinder the war effort, naïve also to deny that the resulting limitation might well lead to a lowering of university standards.[26] The only thing this divorce is not likely to lead to is a general withdrawal of federal funds; for, as Jerome Lettvin, of M.I.T., recently pointed out, "The Government can't afford not to support us" [27]—just as the universities cannot afford not to accept federal funds; but this means no more than that they "must learn how to sterilize financial support" (Henry Steele Commager), a difficult but not impossible task in view of the enormous increase of the power of universities in modern societies.) In short, the seemingly irresistible proliferation of techniques and machines, far from only threatening certain classes with unemployment, menaces the existence of whole nations and conceivably of all mankind.

It is only natural that the new generation should live with greater awareness of the possibility of doomsday than those "over thirty," not because they are younger but because this was their first decisive experience in the world. (What are "problems" to us "are built into the flesh and blood of the young.") [28] If you ask a member of this generation two simple questions: "How do you want the world to be in fifty years?" and "What do you want your life to be like five years from now?" the answers are quite

[25] See appendix V, p. 189.

[26] The steady drift of basic research from the universities to the industrial laboratories is very significant and a case in point.

[27] *Loc. cit.*

[28] Stephen Spender, *The Year of the Young Rebels,* New York, 1969, p. 179.

often preceded by "Provided there is still a world," and "Provided I am still alive." In George Wald's words, "what we are up against is a generation that is by no means sure that it has a future." [29] For the future, as Spender puts it, is "like a time-bomb buried, but ticking away, in the present." To the often-heard question Who are they, this new generation? one is tempted to answer, Those who hear the ticking. And to the other question, Who are they who utterly deny them? the answer may well be, Those who do not know, or refuse to face, things as they really are.

The student rebellion is a global phenomenon, but its manifestations vary, of course, greatly from country to country, often from university to university. This is especially true of the practice of violence. Violence has remained mostly a matter of theory and rhetoric where the clash between generations did not coincide with a clash of tangible group interests. This was notably so in Germany, where the tenured faculty had a vested interest in overcrowded lectures and seminars. In America, the student movement has been seriously radicalized wherever police and police brutality intervened in essentially nonviolent demonstrations: occupations of administration buildings, sit-ins, et cetera. Serious violence entered the scene only with the appearance of the Black Power movement on the campuses. Negro students, the majority of them admitted without academic qualification, regarded and organized themselves as an interest group, the representatives of the black community. Their interest was to lower academic standards. They were more cautious than the white rebels, but it was clear from the beginning (even before the incidents at Cornell University and City College in New York) that violence with them was not a matter of theory and rhetoric. Moreover, while the student rebellion in

[29] George Wald in *The New Yorker*, March 22, 1969.

Western countries can nowhere count on popular support outside the universities and as a rule encounters open hostility the moment it uses violent means, there stands a large minority of the Negro community behind the verbal or actual violence of the black students.[30] Black violence can indeed be understood in analogy to the labor violence in America a generation ago; and although, as far as I know, only Staughton Lynd has drawn the analogy between labor riots and student rebellion explicitly,[31] it seems that the academic establishment, in its curious tendency to yield more to Negro demands, even if they are clearly silly and outrageous,[32] than to the disinterested and usually highly moral claims of the white rebels, also thinks in these terms and feels more comfortable when confronted with interests plus violence than when it is a matter of nonviolent "participatory democracy." The yielding of university authorities to black demands has often been explained by the "guilt feelings" of the white community; I think it is more likely that faculty as well as administrations and boards of trustees are half-consciously aware of the obvious truth of a conclusion of the official *Report on Violence in America:* "Force and violence are likely to be successful techniques of social control and persuasion when they have wide popular support."[33]

The new undeniable glorification of violence by the student movement has a curious peculiarity. While the rheto-

---

[30] See appendix VI, p. 190.

[31] See appendix VII, p. 191.

[32] See appendix VIII, p. 191.

[33] See the report of the *National Commission on the Causes and Prevention of Violence,* June, 1969, as quoted from the New York *Times,* June 6, 1969.

ric of the new militants is clearly inspired by Fanon, their theoretical arguments contain usually nothing but a hodgepodge of all kinds of Marxist leftovers. This is indeed quite baffling for anybody who has ever read Marx or Engels. Who could possibly call an ideology Marxist that has put its faith in "classless idlers," believes that "in the lumpenproletariat the rebellion will find its urban spearhead," and trusts that "gangsters will light the way for the people"? [34] Sartre with his great felicity with words has given expression to the new faith. "Violence," he now believes, on the strength of Fanon's book, "like Achilles' lance, can heal the wounds it has inflicted." If this were true, revenge would be the cure-all for most of our ills. This myth is more abstract, farther removed from reality, than Sorel's myth of a general strike ever was. It is on a par with Fanon's worst rhetorical excesses, such as, "hunger with dignity is preferable to bread eaten in slavery." No history and no theory is needed to refute this statement; the most superficial observer of the processes that go on in the human body knows its untruth. But had he said that bread eaten with dignity is preferable to cake eaten in slavery the rhetorical point would have been lost.

Reading these irresponsible grandiose statements—and those I quoted are fairly representative, except that Fanon still manages to stay closer to reality than most—and looking at them in the perspective of what we know about the history of rebellions and revolutions, one is tempted to deny their significance, to ascribe them to a passing mood, or to the ignorance and nobility of sentiment of people exposed to unprecedented events and developments without any means of handling them mentally, and who therefore curiously revive thoughts and emotions from which Marx had hoped to liberate the revolution once and for all.

---

[34] Fanon, *op. cit.*, pp. 130, 129, and 69, respectively.

Who has ever doubted that the violated dream of violence, that the oppressed "dream at least once a day of setting" themselves up in the oppressor's place, that the poor dream of the possessions of the rich, the persecuted of exchanging "the role of the quarry for that of the hunter," and the last of the kingdom where "the last shall be first, and the first last"? [35] The point, as Marx saw it, is that dreams never come true. [36] The rarity of slave rebellions and of uprisings among the disinherited and downtrodden is notorious; on the few occasions when they occurred it was precisely "mad fury" that turned dreams into nightmares for everybody. In no case, as far as I know, was the force of these "volcanic" outbursts, in Sartre's words, "equal to that of the pressure put on them." To identify the national liberation movements with such outbursts is to prophesy their doom—quite apart from the fact that the unlikely victory would not result in changing the world (or the system), but only its personnel. To think, finally, that there is such a thing as a "Unity of the Third World," to which one could address the new slogan in the era of decolonization "Natives of all underdeveloped countries unite!" (Sartre) is to repeat Marx's worst illusions on a greatly enlarged scale and with considerably less justification. The Third World is not a reality but an ideology. [37]

[35] Fanon, *op. cit.*, pp. 37 ff., 53.

[36] See appendix IX, p. 192.

[37] The students caught between the two superpowers and equally disillusioned by East and West, "inevitably pursue some third ideology, from Mao's China or Castro's Cuba." (Spender, *op. cit.*, p. 92.) Their calls for Mao, Castro, Che Guevara, and Ho Chi Minh are like pseudo-religious incantations for saviors from another world; they would also call for Tito if only Yugoslavia were farther away and less approachable. The case is different with the Black Power movement; its ideological commitment to the nonexistent

The question remains why so many of the new preachers of violence are unaware of their decisive disagreement with Karl Marx's teachings, or, to put it another way, why they cling with such stubborn tenacity to concepts and doctrines that have not only been refuted by factual developments but are clearly inconsistent with their own politics. The one positive political slogan the new movement has put forth, the claim for "participatory democracy" that has echoed around the globe and constitutes the most significant common denominator of the rebellions in the East and the West, derives from the best in the revolutionary tradition—the council system, the always defeated but only authentic outgrowth of every revolution since the eighteenth century. But no reference to this goal either in word or substance can be found in the teachings of Marx and Lenin, both of whom aimed on the contrary at a society in which the need for public action and participation in public affairs would have "withered away," [38]

"Unity of the Third World" is not sheer romantic nonsense.. They have an obvious interest in a black-white dichotomy; this too is of course mere escapism—an escape into a dream world in which Negroes would constitute an overwhelming majority of the world's population.

[38] It seems as though a similar inconsistency could be charged to Marx and Lenin. Did not Marx glorify the Paris Commune of 1871, and did not Lenin want to give "all power to the *soviets*"? But for Marx the Commune was no more than a transitory organ of revolutionary action, "a lever for uprooting the economical foundations of . . . class rule," which Engels rightly identified with the likewise transitory "dictatorship of the Proletariat." (See *The Civil War in France,* in Karl Marx and F. Engels, *Selected Works,* London, 1950, Vol. I, pp. 474 and 440, respectively.) The case of Lenin is more complicated. Still, it was Lenin who emasculated the *soviets* and gave all power to the party.

together with the state. Because of a curious timidity in theoretical matters, contrasting oddly with its bold courage in practice, the slogan of the New Left has remained in a declamatory stage, to be invoked rather inarticulately against Western representative democracy (which is about to lose even its merely representative function to the huge party machines that "represent" not the party membership but its functionaries) and against the Eastern one-party bureaucracies, which rule out participation on principle.

Even more suprising in this odd loyalty to the past is the New Left's seeming unawareness of the extent to which the moral character of the rebellion—now a widely accepted fact [39]—clashes with its Marxian rhetoric. Nothing, indeed, about the movement is more striking than its disinterestedness; Peter Steinfels, in a remarkable article on the "French revolution 1968" in *Commonweal* (July 26, 1968), was quite right when he wrote: "Péguy might have been an appropriate patron for the cultural revolution, with his later scorn for the Sorbonne mandarinate [and] his formula, 'The social Revolution will be moral or it will

---

[39] "Their revolutionary idea," as Spender (*op. cit.*, p. 114) states, "is moral passion." Noam Chomsky (*op. cit.*, p. 368) quotes facts: "The fact is that most of the thousand draft cards and other documents turned in to the Justice Department on October 20 [1967] came from men who can escape military service but who insisted on sharing the fate of those who are less privileged." The same was true for any number of draft-resister demonstrations and sit-ins in the universities and colleges. The situation in other countries is similar. *Der Spiegel* describes, for instance, the frustrating and often humiliating conditions of the research assistants in Germany: "*Angesichts dieser Verhältnisse nimmt es geradezu wunder, dass die Assistenten nicht in der vordersten Front der Radikalen stehen.*" (June 23, 1969, p. 58.) It is always the same story: Interest groups do not join the rebels.

not be.' " To be sure, every revolutionary movement has been led by the disinterested, who were motivated by compassion or by a passion for justice, and this, of course, is also true for Marx and Lenin. But Marx, as we know, had quite effectively tabooed these "emotions"—if today the establishment dismisses moral arguments as "emotionalism" it is much closer to Marxist ideology than the rebels—and had solved the problem of "disinterested" leaders with the notion of their being the vanguard of mankind, embodying the ultimate interest of human history.[40] Still, they too had first to espouse the nonspeculative, down-to-earth interests of the working class and to identify with it; this alone gave them a firm footing outside society. And this is precisely what the modern rebels have lacked from the beginning and have been unable to find despite a rather desperate search for allies outside the universities. The hostility of the workers in all countries is a matter of record,[41] and in the United States the complete collapse of any co-operation with the Black Power movement, whose students are more firmly rooted in their own community and therefore in a better bargaining position at the universities, was the bitterest disappointment for the white rebels. (Whether it was wise of the Black Power people to refuse to play the role of the proletariat for "disinterested" leaders of a different color is another question.) It is, not surprisingly, in Germany, the old home of the Youth movement, that a group of students now proposes

[40] See appendix X, p. 192.

[41] Czechoslovakia seems to be an exception. However, the reform movement for which the students fought in the first ranks was backed by the whole nation, without any class distinctions. Marxistically speaking, the students there, and probably in all Eastern countries, have too much, rather than too little, support from the community to fit the Marxian pattern.

to enlist "all organized youth groups" in their ranks.[42] The absurdity of this proposal is obvious.

I am not sure what the explanation of these inconsistencies will eventually turn out to be; but I suspect that the deeper reason for this loyalty to a typically nineteenth-century doctrine has something to do with the concept of Progress, with an unwillingness to part with a notion that used to unite Liberalism, Socialism, and Communism into the "Left" but has nowhere reached the level of plausibility and sophistication we find in the writings of Karl Marx. (Inconsistency has always been the Achilles' heel of liberal thought; it combined an unswerving loyalty to Progress with a no less strict refusal to glorify History in Marxian and Hegelian terms, which alone could justify and guarantee it.)

The notion that there is such a thing as progress of mankind as a whole was unknown prior to the seventeenth century, developed into a rather common opinion among the eighteenth-century *hommes de lettres,* and became an almost universally accepted dogma in the nineteenth. But the difference between the earlier notions and their final stage is decisive. The seventeenth century, in this respect best represented by Pascal and Fontenelle, thought of progress in terms of an accumulation of knowledge through the centuries, whereas for the eighteenth the word implied an "education of mankind" (Lessing's *Erziehung des Menschengeschlechts*) whose end would coincide with man's coming of age. Progress was not unlimited, and Marx's classless society seen as the realm of freedom that could be the end of history—often interpreted as a secularization of Christian eschatology or Jewish messianism—actually still bears the hallmark of the Age of Enlightenment. Be-

---

[42] See the Spiegel-Interview with Christoph Ehmann in *Der Spiegel,* February 10, 1969.

ginning with the nineteenth century, however, all such limitations disappeared. Now, in the words of Proudhon, motion is *"le fait primitif"* and "the laws of movement alone are eternal." This movement has neither beginning nor end: *"Le mouvement est; voilà tout!"* As to man, all we can say is "we are born perfectible, but we shall never be perfect." [43] Marx's idea, borrowed from Hegel, that every old society harbors the seeds of its successors in the same way every living organism harbors the seeds of its offspring is indeed not only the most ingenious but also the only possible conceptual guarantee for the sempiternal continuity of progress in history; and since the motion of this progress is supposed to come about through the clashes of antagonistic forces, it is possible to interpret every "regress" as a necessary but temporary setback.

To be sure, a guarantee that in the final analysis rests on little more than a metaphor is not the most solid basis to erect a doctrine upon, but this, unhappily, Marxism shares with a great many other doctrines in philosophy. Its great advantage becomes clear as soon as one compares it with other concepts of history—such as "eternal recurrences," the rise and fall of empires, the haphazard sequence of essentially unconnected events—all of which can equally be documented and justified, but none of which will guarantee a continuum of linear time and continuous progress in history. And the only competitor in the field, the ancient notion of a Golden Age at the beginning, from which everything else is derived, implies the rather unpleasant certainty of continuous decline. Of course, there are a few melancholy side effects in the reassuring idea that we need only march into the future,

[43] P.-J. Proudhon, *Philosophie du Progrès* (1853), 1946, pp. 27-30, 49, and *De la Justice* (1858), 1930, I, p. 238, respectively. See also William H. Harbold, "Progressive Humanity: in the Philosophy of P.-J. Proudhon," *Review of Politics*, January, 1969.

which we cannot help doing anyhow, in order to find a better world. There is first of all the simple fact that the general future of mankind has nothing to offer to individual life, whose only certain future is death. And if one leaves this out of account and thinks only in generalities, there is the obvious argument against progress that, in the words of Herzen, "Human development is a form of chronological unfairness, since late-comers are able to profit by the labors of their predecessors without paying the same price," [44] or, in the words of Kant, "It will always remain bewildering . . . that the earlier generations seem to carry on their burdensome business only for the sake of the later . . . and that only the last should have the good fortune to dwell in the [completed] building." [45]

However, these disadvantages, which were only rarely noticed, are more than outweighed by an enormous advantage: progress not only explains the past without breaking up the time continuum but it can serve as a guide for acting into the future. This is what Marx discovered when he turned Hegel upside down: he changed the direction of the historian's glance; instead of looking toward the past, he now could confidently look into the future. Progress gives an answer to the troublesome question, And what shall we do now? The answer, on the lowest level, says: Let us develop what we have into something better, greater, et cetera. (The, at first glance, irrational faith of liberals in growth, so characteristic of all our present political and economic theories, depends on this notion.) On the more sophisticated level of the Left, it tells us to develop present contradictions into their inherent synthesis.

[44] Alexander Herzen is quoted here from Isaiah Berlin's "Introduction" to Franco Venturi, *Roots of Revolutions*, New York, 1966.

[45] "Idea for a Universal History with Cosmopolitan Intent," Third Principle, in *The Philosophy of Kant*, Modern Library edition.

In either case we are assured that nothing altogether new and totally unexpected can happen, nothing but the "necessary" results of what we already know.[46] How reassuring that, in Hegel's words, "nothing else will come out but what was already there." [47]

I do not need to add that all our experiences in this century, which has constantly confronted us with the totally unexpected, stand in flagrant contradiction to these notions and doctrines, whose very popularity seems to consist in offering a comfortable, speculative or pseudo-scientific refuge from reality. A student rebellion almost exclusively inspired by moral considerations certainly belongs among the totally unexpected events of this century. This generation, trained like its predecessors in hardly anything but the various brands of the my-share-of-the-pie social and political theories, has taught us a lesson about manipulation, or, rather, its limits, which we would do well not to forget. Men can be "manipulated" through physical coercion, torture, or starvation, and their opinions can be arbitrarily formed by deliberate, organized misinformation, but not through "hidden persuaders," television, advertising, or any other psychological means in a free society. Alas, refutation of theory through reality has always been at best a lengthy and precarious business. The manipulation addicts, those who fear it unduly no less than those who have set their hopes on it, hardly notice when the chickens come home to roost. (One of the nicest examples of theories exploding into absurdity happened during the recent "People's Park" trouble in Berkeley.

[46] For an excellent discussion of the obvious fallacies in this position, see Robert A. Nisbet, "The Year 2000 and All That," in *Commentary*, June, 1968, and the ill-tempered critical remarks in the September issue.

[47] Hegel, *op. cit.*, p. 100 ff.

When the police and the National Guard, with rifles, unsheathed bayonets, and helicoptered riot gas, attacked the unarmed students—few of them "had thrown anything more dangerous than epithets"—some Guardsmen fraternized openly with their "enemies" and one of them threw down his arms and shouted: "I can't stand this any more." What happened? In the enlightened age we live in, this could be explained only by insanity; "he was rushed to a psychiatric examination [and] diagnosed as suffering from 'suppressed aggressions.' ") [48]

Progress, to be sure, is a more serious and a more complex item offered at the superstition fair of our time.[49] The irrational nineteenth-century belief in *unlimited* progress has found universal acceptance chiefly because of the astounding development of the natural sciences, which, since the rise of the modern age, actually have been "universal" sciences and therefore could look forward to an unending task in exploring the immensity of the universe. That science, even though no longer limited by the finitude of the earth and its nature, should be subject to never-ending progress is by no means certain; that strictly scientific research in the humanities, the so-called *Geisteswissenschaften* that deal with the products of the human spirit, must come to an end by definition is obvious. The ceaseless, senseless demand for original scholarship in a number of fields, where only erudition is now possible, has

[48] The incident is reported without comment by Wolin and Schaar, *op. cit.* See also Peter Barnes's report " 'An Outcry': Thoughts on Being Tear Gassed," in *Newsweek*, June 2, 1969.

[49] Spender (*op. cit.*, p. 45) reports that the French students during the May incidents in Paris "refused categorically the ideology of 'output' [*rendement*], of 'progress' and such-called pseudo-forces." In America, this is not yet the case as far as progress is concerned. We are still surrounded by talk about "progressive" and "regressive" forces, "progressive" and "repressive tolerance," and the like.

led either to sheer irrelevancy, the famous knowing of more and more about less and less, or to the development of a pseudo-scholarship which actually destroys its object.[50] It is noteworthy that the rebellion of the young, to the extent that it is not exclusively morally or politically motivated, has been chiefly directed against the academic glorification of scholarship and science, both of which, though for different reasons, are gravely compromised in their eyes. And it is true that it is by no means impossible that we have reached in both cases a turning point, the point of destructive returns. Not only has the progress of science ceased to coincide with the progress of mankind (whatever that may mean), but it could even spell mankind's end, just as the further progress of scholarship may well end with the destruction of everything that made scholarship worth our while. Progress, in other words, can no longer serve as the standard by which to evaluate the disastrously rapid change-processes we have let loose.

Since we are concerned here primarily with violence, I must warn against a tempting misunderstanding. If we look on history in terms of a continuous chronological process, whose progress, moreover, is inevitable, violence in the shape of war and revolution may appear to constitute the only possible interruption. If this were true, if only the practice of violence would make it possible to interrupt automatic processes in the realm of human affairs, the preachers of violence would have won an important point. (Theoretically, as far as I know, the point was never made, but it seems to me incontestable that the disruptive student activities in the last few years are actually based on this conviction.) It is the function, how-

---

[50] For a splendid exemplification of these not merely superfluous but pernicious enterprises, see Edmund Wilson, *The Fruits of the MLA,* New York, 1968.

ever, of all action, as distinguished from mere behavior, to interrupt what otherwise would have proceeded automatically and therefore predictably.

II

I T I S against the background of these experiences that I propose to raise the question of violence in the political realm. This is not easy; what Sorel remarked sixty years ago, "The problems of violence still remain very obscure," [51] is as true today as it was then. I mentioned the general reluctance to deal with violence as a phenomenon in its own right, and I must now qualify this statement. If we turn to discussions of the phenomenon of power, we soon find that there exists a consensus among political theorists from Left to Right to the effect that violence is nothing more than the most flagrant manifestation of power. "All politics is a struggle for power; the ultimate kind of power is violence," said C. Wright Mills, echoing, as it were, Max Weber's definition of the state as "the rule of men over men based on the means of legitimate, that is allegedly legitimate, violence." [52] The consensus is very

---

[51] Georges Sorel, *Reflections on Violence,* "Introduction to the First Publication" (1906), New York, 1961, p. 60.

[52] *The Power Elite,* New York, 1956, p. 171; Max Weber in the first paragraphs of *Politics as a Vocation* (1921). Weber seems to have been aware of his agreement with the Left. He quotes in the context Trotsky's remark in Brest-Litovsk, "Every state is based on violence," and adds, "This is indeed true."

strange; for to equate political power with "the organization of violence" makes sense only if one follows Marx's estimate of the state as an instrument of oppression in the hands of the ruling class. Let us therefore turn to authors who do not believe that the body politic and its laws and institutions are merely coercive superstructures, secondary manifestations of some underlying forces. Let us turn, for instance, to Bertrand de Jouvenel, whose book *Power* is perhaps the most prestigious and, anyway, the most interesting recent treatise on the subject. "To him," he writes, "who contemplates the unfolding of the ages war presents itself as an activity of States *which pertains to their essence.*" [53] This may prompt us to ask whether the end of warfare, then, would mean the end of states. Would the disappearance of violence in relationships between states spell the end of power?

The answer, it seems, will depend on what we understand by power. And power, it turns out, is an instrument of rule, while rule, we are told, owes its existence to "the instinct of domination." [54] We are immediately reminded of what Sartre said about violence when we read in Jouvenel that "a man feels himself more of a man when he is imposing himself and making others the instruments of his will," which gives him "incomparable pleasure." [55] "Power," said Voltaire, "consists in making others act as I choose"; it is present wherever I have the chance "to assert my own will against the resistance" of others, said Max Weber, reminding us of Clausewitz's definition of war as "an act of violence to compel the opponent to do as we wish." The word, we are told by Strausz-Hupé, signifies

[53] *Power: The Natural History of Its Growth* (1945), London, 1952, p. 122.

[54] *Ibidem,* p. 93.

[55] *Ibidem,* p. 110.

"the power of man over man." [56] To go back to Jouvenel: "To command and to be obeyed: without that, there is no Power—with it no other attribute is needed for it to be. . . . The thing without which it cannot be: that essence is command." [57] If the essence of power is the effectiveness of command, then there is no greater power than that which grows out of the barrel of a gun, and it would be difficult to say in "which way the order given by a policeman is different from that given by a gunman." (I am quoting from the important book *The Notion of the State*, by Alexander Passerin d'Entrèves, the only author I know who is aware of the importance of distinguishing between violence and power. "We have to decide whether and in what sense 'power' can be distinguished from 'force', to ascertain how the fact of using force according to law changes the quality of force itself and presents us with an entirely different picture of human relations," since "force, by the very fact of being qualified, ceases to be force." But even this distinction, by far the most sophisticated and thoughtful one in the literature, does not go

[56] See Karl von Clausewitz, *On War* (1832), New York, 1943, ch. 1; Robert Strausz-Hupé, *Power and Community*, New York, 1956, p. 4; the quotation from Max Weber: *"Macht bedeutet jede Chance, innerhalb einer sozialen Beziehung den eigenen Willen auch gegen Widerstand durchzusetzen,"* is drawn from Strausz-Hupé.

[57] I chose my examples at random, since it hardly matters to which author one turns. It is only occasionally that one hears a dissenting voice. Thus R. M. McIver states, "Coercive power is a criterion of the state, but not its essence. . . . It is true that there is no state, where there is no overwhelming force. . . . But the exercise of force does not make a state." (In *The Modern State*, London, 1926, pp. 222-225.) How strong the force of this tradition is can be seen in Rousseau's attempt to escape it. Looking for a government of no-rule, he finds nothing better than *"une forme d'association . . . par laquelle chacun s'unissant à tous n'obéisse pourtant qu'à lui-même."* The emphasis on obedience, and hence on command, is unchanged.

to the root of the matter. Power in Passerin d'Entrèves's understanding is "qualified" or "institutionalized force." In other words, while the authors quoted above define violence as the most flagrant manifestation of power, Passerin d'Entrèves defines power as a kind of mitigated violence. In the final analysis, it comes to the same.) [58] Should everybody from Right to Left, from Bertrand de Jouvenel to Mao Tse-tung agree on so basic a point in political philosophy as the nature of power?

In terms of our traditions of political thought, these definitions have much to recommend them. Not only do they derive from the old notion of absolute power that accompanied the rise of the sovereign European nation-state, whose earliest and still greatest spokesmen were Jean Bodin, in sixteenth-century France, and Thomas Hobbes, in seventeenth-century England; they also coincide with the terms used since Greek antiquity to define the forms of government as the rule of man over man—of one or the few in monarchy and oligarchy, of the best or the many in aristocracy and democracy. Today we ought to add the latest and perhaps most formidable form of such dominion: bureaucracy or the rule of an intricate system of bureaus in which no men, neither one nor the best, neither the few nor the many, can be held responsible, and which could be properly called rule by Nobody. (If, in accord with traditional political thought, we identify tyranny as government that is not held to give account of itself, rule by Nobody is clearly the most tyrannical of all, since there is no one left who could even be asked to answer for what

[58] *The Notion of the State, An Introduction to Political Theory* was first published in Italian in 1962. The English version is no mere translation; written by the author himself, it is the definitive edition and appeared in Oxford in 1967. For the quotations, see pp. 64, 70, and 105.

is being done. It is this state of affairs, making it impossible to localize responsibility and to identify the enemy, that is among the most potent causes of the current worldwide rebellious unrest, its chaotic nature, and its dangerous tendency to get out of control and to run amuck.)

Moreover, this ancient vocabulary was strangely confirmed and fortified by the addition of the Hebrew-Christian tradition and its "imperative conception of law." This concept was not invented by the "political realists" but was, rather, the result of a much earlier, almost automatic generalization of God's "Commandments," according to which "the simple relation of command and obedience" indeed sufficed to identify the essence of law.[59] Finally, more modern scientific and philosophical convictions concerning man's nature have further strengthened these legal and political traditions. The many recent discoveries of an inborn instinct of domination and an innate aggressiveness in the human animal were preceded by very similar philosophic statements. According to John Stuart Mill, "the first lesson of civilization [is] that of obedience," and he speaks of "the two states of the inclinations . . . one the desire to exercise power over others; the other . . . disinclination to have power exercised over themselves." [60] If we would trust our own experiences in these matters, we should know that the instinct of submission, an ardent desire to obey and be ruled by some strong man, is at least as prominent in human psychology as the will to power, and, politically, perhaps more relevant. The old adage "How fit he is to sway / That can so well obey," some version of which seems to have been

[59] *Ibidem*, p. 129.

[60] *Considerations on Representative Government* (1861), Liberal Arts Library, pp. 59 and 65.

138

known to all centuries and all nations,[61] may point to a psychological truth: namely, that the will to power and the will to submission are interconnected. "Ready submission to tyranny," to use Mill once more, is by no means always caused by "extreme passiveness." Conversely, a strong disinclination to obey is often accompanied by an equally strong disinclination to dominate and command. Historically speaking, the ancient institution of slave economy would be inexplicable on the grounds of Mill's psychology. Its express purpose was to liberate citizens from the burden of household affairs and to permit them to enter the public life of the community, where all were equals; if it were true that nothing is sweeter than to give commands and to rule others, the master would never have left his household.

However, there exists another tradition and another vocabulary no less old and time-honored. When the Athenian city-state called its constitution an isonomy, or the Romans spoke of the *civitas* as their form of government, they had in mind a concept of power and law whose essence did not rely on the command-obedience relationship and which did not identify power and rule or law and command. It was to these examples that the men of the eighteenth-century revolutions turned when they ransacked the archives of antiquity and constituted a form of government, a republic, where the rule of law, resting on the power of the people, would put an end to the rule of man over man, which they thought was a "government fit for slaves." They too, unhappily, still talked about obedience—obedience to laws instead of men; but what they actually meant was support of the laws to which the

---

[61] John M. Wallace, *Destiny His Choice: The Loyalism of Andrew Marvell*, Cambridge, 1968, pp. 88-89. I owe this reference to the kind attention of Gregory DesJardins.

citizenry had given its consent.[62] Such support is never unquestioning, and as far as reliability is concerned it cannot match the indeed "unquestioning obedience" that an act of violence can exact—the obedience every criminal can count on when he snatches my pocketbook with the help of a knife or robs a bank with the help of a gun. It is the people's support that lends power to the institutions of a country, and this support is but the continuation of the consent that brought the laws into existence to begin with Under conditions of representative government the people are supposed to rule those who govern them. All political institutions are manifestations and materializations of power; they petrify and decay as soon as the living power of the people ceases to uphold them. This is what Madison meant when he said "all governments rest on opinion," a word no less true for the various forms of monarchy than for democracies. ("To suppose that majority rule functions only in democracy is a fantastic illusion," as Jouvenel points out: "The king, who is but one solitary individual, stands far more in need of the general support of Society than any other form of government." [63] Even the tyrant, the One who rules against all, needs helpers in the business of violence, though their number may be rather restricted.) However, the strength of opinion, that is, the power of the government, depends on numbers; it is "in proportion to the number with which it is associated," [64] and tyranny, as Montesquieu discovered, is therefore the most violent and least powerful of forms of government. Indeed one of the most obvious distinctions between power and violence is that

[62] See appendix XI, p. 193.

[63] *Op. cit.*, p. 98.

[64] *The Federalist*. No. 49.

power always stands in need of numbers, whereas violence up to a point can manage without them because it relies on implements. A legally unrestricted majority rule, that is, a democracy without a constitution, can be very formidable in the suppression of the rights of minorities and very effective in the suffocation of dissent without any use of violence. But that does not mean that violence and power are the same.

The extreme form of power is All against One, the extreme form of violence is One against All. And this latter is never possible without instruments. To claim, as is often done, that a tiny unarmed minority has successfully, by means of violence—shouting, kicking up a row, et cetera—disrupted large lecture classes whose overwhelming majority had voted for normal instruction procedures is therefore very misleading. (In a recent case at some German university there was even one lonely "dissenter" among several hundred students who could claim such a strange victory.) What actually happens in such cases is something much more serious: the majority clearly refuses to use its power and overpower the disrupters; the academic processes break down because no one is willing to raise more than a voting finger for the *status quo*. What the universities are up against is the "immense negative unity" of which Stephen Spender speaks in another context. All of which proves only that a minority can have a much greater potential power than one would expect by counting noses in public-opinion polls. The merely onlooking majority, amused by the spectacle of a shouting match between student and professor, is in fact already the latent ally of the minority. (One need only imagine what would have happened had one or a few unarmed Jews in pre-Hitler Germany tried to disrupt the lecture of an anti-Semitic professor in order to understand the absurdity of the talk about the small "minorities of militants.")

It is, I think, a rather sad reflection on the present state of political science that our terminology does not distinguish among such key words as "power," "strength," "force," "authority," and, finally, "violence"—all of which refer to distinct, different phenomena and would hardly exist unless they did. (In the words of d'Entrèves, "might, power, authority: these are all words to whose exact implications no great weight is attached in current speech; even the greatest thinkers sometimes use them at random. Yet it is fair to presume that they refer to different properties, and their meaning should therefore be carefully assessed and examined. . . . The correct use of these words is a question not only of logical grammar, but of historical perspective.") [65] To use them as synonyms not only indicates a certain deafness to linguistic meanings, which would be serious enough, but it has also resulted in a kind of blindness to the realities they correspond to. In such a situation it is always tempting to introduce new definitions, but—though I shall briefly yield to temptation—what is involved is not simply a matter of careless speech. Behind the apparent confusion is a firm conviction in whose light all distinctions would be, at best, of minor importance: the conviction that the most crucial political issue is, and always has been, the question of Who rules Whom? Power, strength, force, authority, violence—these are but words to indicate the means by which man rules over man; they are held to be synonyms because they have the same function. It is only after one

[65] *Op. cit.*, p. 7. Cf. also p. 171, where, discussing the exact meaning of the words "nation" and "nationality," he rightly insists that "the only competent guides in the jungle of so many different meanings are the linguists and the historians. It is to them that we must turn for help." And in distinguishing authority and power, he turns to Cicero's *potestas in populo, auctoritas in senatu.*

ceases to reduce public affairs to the business of dominion that the original data in the realm of human affairs will appear, or, rather, reappear, in their authentic diversity.

These data, in our context, may be enumerated as follows:

Power corresponds to the human ability not just to act but to act in concert. Power is never the property of an individual; it belongs to a group and remains in existence only so long as the group keeps together. When we say of somebody that he is "in power" we actually refer to his being empowered by a certain number of people to act in their name. The moment the group, from which the power originated to begin with (*potestas in populo*, without a people or group there is no power), disappears, "his power" also vanishes. In current usage, when we speak of a "powerful man" or a "powerful personality," we already use the word "power" metaphorically; what we refer to without metaphor is "strength."

Strength unequivocally designates something in the singular, an individual entity; it is the property inherent in an object or person and belongs to its character, which may prove itself in relation to other things or persons, but is essentially independent of them. The strength of even the strongest individual can always be overpowered by the many, who often will combine for no other purpose than to ruin strength precisely because of its peculiar independence. The almost instinctive hostility of the many toward the one has always, from Plato to Nietzsche, been ascribed to resentment, to the envy of the weak for the strong, but this psychological interpretation misses the point. It is in the nature of a group and its power to turn against independence, the property of individual strength.

Force, which we often use in daily speech as a synonym for violence, especially if violence serves as a means of coercion, should be reserved, in terminological language, for the "forces of nature" or the "force of circumstances" (*la force des choses*), that is, to indicate the energy released by physical or social movements.

Authority, relating to the most elusive of these phenomena and therefore, as a term, most frequently abused,[66] can be vested in persons—there is such a thing as personal authority, as, for instance, in the relation between parent and child, between teacher and pupil—or it can be vested in offices, as, for instance, in the Roman senate (*auctoritas in senatu*) or in the hierarchical offices of the Church (a priest can grant valid absolution even though he is drunk). Its hallmark is unquestioning recognition by those who are asked to obey; neither coercion nor persuasion is needed. (A father can lose his authority either by beating his child or by starting to argue with him, that is, either by behaving to him like a tyrant or by treating him as an equal.) To remain in authority requires respect for the person or the office. The greatest enemy of authority, therefore, is contempt, and the surest way to undermine it is laughter.[67]

[66] There is such a thing as authoritarian government, but it certainly has nothing in common with tyranny, dictatorship, or totalitarian rule. For a discussion of the historical background and political significance of the term, see my "What is Authority?" in *Between Past and Future: Exercises in Political Thought*, New York, 1968, and Part I of Karl-Heinz Lübke's valuable study, *Auctoritas bei Augustin*, Stuttgart, 1968, with extensive bibliography.

[67] Wolin and Schaar, in *op. cit.*, are entirely right: "The rules are being broken because University authorities, administrators and faculty alike, have lost the respect of many of the students." They then conclude, "When authority leaves, power enters." This too is true, but, I am afraid, not quite in the sense they meant it. What entered first at Berkeley was student power, obviously the strongest power on every campus simply because of the students' superior numbers. It was in order to break this power that authorities resorted to violence, and it is precisely because the university is essentially an institution based on authority, and therefore in need

Violence, finally, as I have said, is distinguished by its instrumental character. Phenomenologically, it is close to strength, since the implements of violence, like all other tools, are designed and used for the purpose of multiplying natural strength until, in the last stage of their development, they can substitute for it.

It is perhaps not superfluous to add that these distinctions, though by no means arbitrary, hardly ever correspond to watertight compartments in the real world, from which nevertheless they are drawn. Thus institutionalized power in organized communities often appears in the guise of authority, demanding instant, unquestioning recognition; no society could function without it. (A small, and still isolated, incident in New York shows what can happen if authentic authority in social relations has broken down to the point where it cannot work any longer even in its derivative, purely functional form. A minor mishap in the subway system—the doors on a train failed to operate—turned into a serious shutdown on the line lasting four hours and involving more than fifty thousand passengers, because when the transit authorities asked the passengers to leave the defective train, they simply refused.) [68] Moreover, nothing, as we shall see, is

---

of respect, that it finds it so difficult to deal with power in nonviolent terms. The university today calls upon the police for protection exactly as the Catholic church used to do before the separation of state and church forced it to rely on authority alone. It is perhaps more than an oddity that the severest crisis of the church as an institution should coincide with the severest crisis in the history of the university, the only secular institution still based on authority. Both may indeed be ascribed to "the progressing explosion of the atom 'obedience' whose stability was allegedly eternal," as Heinrich Böll remarked of the crisis in the churches. See "Es wird immer später," in *Antwort an Sacharow,* Zürich, 1969.

[68] See the New York *Times,* January 4, 1969, pp. 1 and 29.

more common than the combination of violence and power, nothing less frequent than to find them in their pure and therefore extreme form. From this, it does not follow that authority, power, and violence are all the same.

Still it must be admitted that it is particularly tempting to think of power in terms of command and obedience, and hence to equate power with violence, in a discussion of what actually is only one of power's special cases—namely, the power of government. Since in foreign relations as well as domestic affairs violence appears as a last resort to keep the power structure intact against individual challengers—the foreign enemy, the native criminal—it looks indeed as though violence were the prerequisite of power and power nothing but a façade, the velvet glove which either conceals the iron hand or will turn out to belong to a paper tiger. On closer inspection, though, this notion loses much of its plausibility. For our purpose, the gap between theory and reality is perhaps best illustrated by the phenomenon of revolution.

Since the beginning of the century theoreticians of revolution have told us that the chances of revolution have significantly decreased in proportion to the increased destructive capacities of weapons at the unique disposition of governments.[69] The history of the last seventy years,

[69] Thus Franz Borkenau, reflecting on the defeat of the Spanish revolution, states: "In this tremendous contrast with previous revolutions one fact is reflected. Before these latter years, counter-revolution usually depended upon the support of reactionary powers, which were technically and intellectually inferior to the forces of revolution. This has changed with the advent of fascism. Now, every revolution is likely to meet the attack of the most modern, most efficient, most ruthless machinery yet in existence. It means that the age of revolutions free to evolve according to their own laws is over." This was written more than thirty years ago (*The Spanish*

with its extraordinary record of successful and unsuccessful revolutions, tells a different story. Were people mad who even tried against such overwhelming odds? And, leaving out instances of full success, how can even a temporary success be explained? The fact is that the gap between state-owned means of violence and what people can muster by themselves—from beer bottles to Molotov cocktails and guns—has always been so enormous that technical improvements make hardly any difference. Textbook instructions on "how to make a revolution" in a step-by-step progression from dissent to conspiracy, from resistance to armed uprising, are all based on the mistaken notion that revolutions are "made." In a contest of violence against violence the superiority of the government has always been absolute; but this superiority lasts only as long as the power structure of the government is intact—that is, as long as commands are obeyed and the army or police forces are prepared to use their weapons. When this is no longer the case, the situation changes abruptly. Not only is the rebellion not put down, but the arms themselves change hands—sometimes, as in the Hungarian revolution, within a few hours. (We should know about such things after all these years of futile fighting in Vietnam, where for a long time, before getting massive Russian aid, the National Liberation Front fought us with weapons that were made in the United States.) Only after this has happened, when the disintegration of the government in power has permitted the rebels to arm themselves, can one speak of an "armed uprising," which often does not

---

Cockpit, London, 1937; Ann Arbor, 1963, pp. 288-289) and is now quoted with approval by Chomsky (*op. cit.,* p. 310). He believes that American and French intervention in the civil war in Vietnam proves Borkenau's prediction accurate, "with substitution of 'liberal imperialism' for 'fascism.' " I think that this example is rather apt to prove the opposite.

take place at all or occurs when it is no longer necessary. Where commands are no longer obeyed, the means of violence are of no use; and the question of this obedience is not decided by the command-obedience relation but by opinion, and, of course, by the number of those who share it. Everything depends on the power behind the violence. The sudden dramatic breakdown of power that ushers in revolutions reveals in a flash how civil obedience —to laws, to rulers, to institutions—is but the outward manifestation of support and consent.

Where power has disintegrated, revolutions are possible but not necessary. We know of many instances when utterly impotent regimes were permitted to continue in existence for long periods of time—either because there was no one to test their strength and reveal their weakness or because they were lucky enough not to be engaged in war and suffer defeat. Disintegration often becomes manifest only in direct confrontation; and even then, when power is already in the street, some group of men prepared for such an eventuality is needed to pick it up and assume responsibility. We have recently witnessed how it did not take more than the relatively harmless, essentially nonviolent French students' rebellion to reveal the vulnerability of the whole political system, which rapidly disintegrated before the astonished eyes of the young rebels. Unknowingly they had tested it; they intended only to challenge the ossified university system, and down came the system of governmental power, together with that of the huge party bureaucracies—*"une sorte de désintégration de toutes les hiérarchies."* [70] It was a textbook case of a revolutionary situation [71] that did not develop into a revo-

[70] Raymond Aron, *La Révolution Introuvable*, 1968, p. 41.

[71] Stephen Spender, *op. cit.*, p. 56, disagrees: "What was so much more apparent than the revolutionary situation [was] the nonrevolutionary one." It may be "difficult to think of a revolution

lution because there was nobody, least of all the students, prepared to seize power and the responsibility that goes with it. Nobody except, of course, de Gaulle. Nothing was more characteristic of the seriousness of the situation than his appeal to the army, his journey to see Massu and the generals in Germany, a walk to Canossa, if there ever was one, in view of what had happened only a few years before. But what he sought and received was support, not obedience, and the means were not commands but concessions.[72] If commands had been enough, he would never have had to leave Paris.

No government exclusively based on the means of violence has ever existed. Even the totalitarian ruler, whose chief instrument of rule is torture, needs a power basis—the secret police and its net of informers. Only the development of robot soldiers, which, as previously mentioned, would eliminate the human factor completely and, conceivably, permit one man with a push button to destroy whomever he pleased, could change this fundamental ascendancy of power over violence. Even the most despotic domination we know of, the rule of master over slaves, who always outnumbered him, did not rest on superior means of coercion as such, but on a superior organization of power—that is, on the organized solidarity of the masters.[73] Single men without others to support them never

---

taking place when . . . everyone looks particularly good humoured," but this is what usually happens in the beginning of revolutions—during the early great ecstasy of fraternity.

[72] See appendix XII, p. 194.

[73] In ancient Greece, such an organization of power was the polis, whose chief merit, according to Xenophon, was that it permitted the "citizens to act as bodyguards to one another against slaves and criminals so that none of the citizens may die a violent death." (*Hiero*, IV, 3.)

have enough power to use violence successfully. Hence, in domestic affairs, violence functions as the last resort of power against criminals or rebels—that is, against single individuals who, as it were, refuse to be overpowered by the consensus of the majority. And as for actual warfare, we have seen in Vietnam how an enormous superiority in the means of violence can become helpless if confronted with an ill-equipped but well-organized opponent who is much more powerful. This lesson, to be sure, was there to be learned from the history of guerrilla warfare, which is at least as old as the defeat in Spain of Napoleon's still-unvanquished army.

To switch for a moment to conceptual language: Power is indeed of the essence of all government, but violence is not. Violence is by nature instrumental; like all means, it always stands in need of guidance and justification through the end it pursues. And what needs justification by something else cannot be the essence of anything. The end of war—end taken in its twofold meaning—is peace or victory; but to the question And what is the end of peace? there is no answer. Peace is an absolute, even though in recorded history periods of warfare have nearly always outlasted periods of peace. Power is in the same category; it is, as they say, "an end in itself." (This, of course, is not to deny that governments pursue policies and employ their power to achieve prescribed goals. But the power structure itself precedes and outlasts all aims, so that power, far from being the means to an end, is actually the very condition enabling a group of people to think and act in terms of the means-end category.) And since government is essentially organized and institutionalized power, the current question What is the end of government? does not make much sense either. The answer will be either question-begging—to enable men to live together—or dangerously utopian—to promote happiness or to realize a classless society or some other nonpolitical ideal, which if tried out in earnest cannot but end in some kind of tyranny.

Power needs no justification, being inherent in the very existence of political communities; what it does need is legitimacy. The common treatment of these two words as synonyms is no less misleading and confusing than the current equation of obedience and support. Power springs up whenever people get together and act in concert, but it derives its legitimacy from the initial getting together rather than from any action that then may follow. Legitimacy, when challenged, bases itself on an appeal to the past, while justification relates to an end that lies in the future. Violence can be justifiable, but it never will be legitimate. Its justification loses in plausibility the farther its intended end recedes into the future. No one questions the use of violence in self-defense, because the danger is not only clear but also present, and the end justifying the means is immediate.

Power and violence, though they are distinct phenomena, usually appear together. Wherever they are combined, power, we have found, is the primary and predominant factor. The situation, however, is entirely different when we deal with them in their pure states—as, for instance, with foreign invasion and occupation. We saw that the current equation of violence with power rests on government's being understood as domination of man over man by means of violence. If a foreign conqueror is confronted by an impotent government and by a nation unused to the exercise of political power, it is easy for him to achieve such domination. In all other cases the difficulties are great indeed, and the occupying invader will try immediately to establish Quisling governments, that is, to find a native power base to support his dominion. The head-on clash between Russian tanks and the entirely nonviolent resistance of the Czechoslovak people is a text-book case of a confrontation between violence and power in their pure states. But while domination in such an instance is difficult to achieve, it is not impossible. Violence, we must remember, does not depend on numbers or opinions, but on implements, and the implements of violence, as I mentioned before, like all other tools, increase and multiply human strength. Those who oppose violence with mere power will soon find that they are confronted not by men but by men's artifacts, whose inhumanity and destructive effectiveness increase in proportion to the distance separating the opponents. Violence can always destroy power; out of the barrel of a gun grows the most effective command, resulting in the most instant and perfect obedience. What never can grow out of it is power.

In a head-on clash between violence and power, the outcome is hardly in doubt. If Gandhi's enormously powerful and successful strategy of nonviolent resistance had met with a different enemy—Stalin's Russia, Hitler's Germany, even prewar Japan, instead of England—the outcome would not have been decolonization, but massacre and submission. However, England in India and France in Algeria had good reasons for their restraint. Rule by sheer violence comes into play where power is being lost; it is precisely the shrinking power of the Russian government, internally and externally, that became manifest in its "solution" of the Czechoslovak problem—just as it was the shrinking power of European imperialism that became manifest in the alternative between decolonization and massacre. To substitute violence for power can bring victory, but the price is very high; for it is not only paid by the vanquished, it is also paid by the victor in terms of his own power. This is especially true when the victor happens to enjoy domestically the bless-

ings of constitutional government. Henry Steele Commager
is entirely right: "If we subvert world order and destroy
world peace we must inevitably subvert and destroy our
own political institutions first." [74] The much-feared boom-
erang effect of the "government of subject races" (Lord
Cromer) on the home government during the imperialist
era meant that rule by violence in faraway lands would
end by affecting the government of England, that the last
"subject race" would be the English themselves. The
recent gas attack on the campus at Berkeley, where not
just tear gas but also another gas, "outlawed by the
Geneva Convention and used by the Army to flush out
guerrillas in Vietnam," was laid down while gas-masked
Guardsmen stopped anybody and everybody "from fleeing
the gassed area," is an excellent example of this "backlash" phenomenon. It has often been said that impotence
breeds violence, and psychologically this is quite true, at
least of persons possessing natural strength, moral or physical. Politically speaking, the point is that loss of power
becomes a temptation to substitute violence for power—in
1968 during the Democratic convention in Chicago we
could watch this process on television [75]—and that violence
itself results in impotence. Where violence is no longer
backed and restrained by power, the well-known reversal
in reckoning with means and ends has taken place. The
means, the means of destruction, now determine the end—
with the consequence that the end will be the destruction
of all power.

Nowhere is the self-defeating factor in the victory of
violence over power more evident than in the use of
terror to maintain domination, about whose weird suc-

[74] "Can We Limit Presidential Power?" in *The New Republic*, April
6, 1968.

[75] See appendix XIII, p. 98.

cesses and eventual failures we know perhaps more than any generation before us. Terror is not the same as violence; it is, rather, the form of government that comes into being when violence, having destroyed all power, does not abdicate but, on the contrary, remains in full control. It has often been noticed that the effectiveness of terror depends almost entirely on the degree of social atomization. Every kind of organized opposition must disappear before the full force of terror can be let loose. This atomization— an outrageously pale, academic word for the horror it implies—is maintained and intensified through the ubiquity of the informer, who can be literally omnipresent because he no longer is merely a professional agent in the pay of the police but potentially every person one comes into contact with. How such a fully developed police state is established and how it works—or, rather, how nothing works where it holds sway—can now be learned in Aleksandr I. Solzhenitsyn's *The First Circle,* which will probably remain one of the masterpieces of twentieth-century literature and certainly contains the best documentation on Stalin's regime in existence.[76] The decisive difference between totalitarian domination, based on terror, and tyrannies and dictatorships, established by violence, is that the former turns not only against its enemies but against its friends and supporters as well, being afraid of all power, even the power of its friends. The climax of terror is reached when the police state begins to devour its own children, when yesterday's executioner becomes today's victim. And this is also the moment when power disappears entirely. There exist now a great many plausible explanations for the de-Stalinization of Russia—none, I believe, so compelling as the realization by the Stalinist functionaries themselves that a continua-

[76] See appendix XIV, p. 195.

tion of the regime would lead, not to an insurrection, against which terror is indeed the best safeguard, but to paralysis of the whole country.

To sum up: politically speaking, it is insufficient to say that power and violence are not the same. Power and violence are opposites; where the one rules absolutely, the other is absent. Violence appears where power is in jeopardy, but left to its own course it ends in power's disappearance. This implies that it is not correct to think of the opposite of violence as nonviolence; to speak of nonviolent power is actually redundant. Violence can destroy power; it is utterly incapable of creating it. Hegel's and Marx's great trust in the dialectial "power of negation," by virtue of which opposites do not destroy but smoothly develop into each other because contradictions promote and do not paralyze development, rests on a much older philosophical prejudice: that evil is no more than a privative *modus* of the good, that good can come out of evil; that, in short, evil is but a temporary manifestation of a still-hidden good. Such time-honored opinions have become dangerous. They are shared by many who have never heard of Hegel or Marx, for the simple reason that they inspire hope and dispel fear—a treacherous hope used to dispel legitimate fear. By this, I do not mean to equate violence with evil; I only want to stress that violence cannot be derived from its opposite, which is power, and that in order to understand it for what it is, we shall have to examine its roots and nature.

III

TO SPEAK about the nature and causes of violence in these terms must appear presumptuous at a moment when floods of foundation money are channeled into the various research projects of social scientists, when a deluge of books on the subject has already appeared, when eminent natural scientists—biologists, physiologists, ethologists, and zoologists—have joined in an all-out effort to solve the riddle of "aggressiveness" in human behavior, and even a brand-new science, called "polemology," has emerged. I have two excuses for trying nevertheless.

First, while I find much of the work of the zoologists fascinating, I fail to see how it can possibly apply to our problem. In order to know that people will fight for their homeland we hardly had to discover instincts of "group territorialism" in ants, fish, and apes; and in order to learn that overcrowding results in irritation and aggressiveness, we hardly needed to experiment with rats. One day spent in the slums of any big city should have sufficed. I am surprised and often delighted to see that some animals behave like men; I cannot see how this could either justify or condemn human behavior. I fail to understand why we are asked "to recognize that man behaves very much like a group territorial species," rather than the other way round—that certain animal species behave very much like men.[77] (Following Adolf Portmann, these new insights into animal behavior do not close the gap between man and animal; they only demonstrate that "much more of what we know of ourselves than we thought also occurs in animals.") [78] Why should we, after having "eliminated" all anthropomorphisms from animal psychology (whether we actually succeeded is another matter), now try to discover "how 'theriomorph' man is"? [79] Is it not obvious that anthropomorphism and theriomorphism in the behavioral sciences are but two sides of the same "error"? Moreover, if we define man as belonging to the animal kingdom, why should we ask him to take his standards of behavior from another animal species? The answer, I am afraid, is simple: It is easier to experiment with animals, and this not only for humanitarian reasons—that it is not nice to put us into cages; the trouble is men can cheat.

Second, the research results of both the social and the natural sciences tend to make violent behavior even more of a "natural" reaction than we would have been prepared to grant without them. Aggressiveness, defined as an instinctual drive, is said to play the same functional role

[77] Nikolas Tinbergen, "On War and Peace in Animals and Man," in *Science*, 160: 1411 (June 28, 1968).

[78] *Das Tier als soziales Wesen*, Zürich, 1953, pp. 237-238: *"Wer sich in die Tatsachen vertieft . . . der wird feststellen, dass die neuen Einblicke in die Differenziertheit tierischen Treibens uns zwingen, mit allzu einfachen Vorstellungen von höheren Tieren ganz entschieden aufzuräumen. Damit wird aber nicht etwa—wie zuweilen leichthin gefolgert wird—das Tierische dem Menschlichen immer mehr genähert. Es zeigt sich lediglich, dass viel mehr von dem, was wir von uns selbst kennen, auch beim Tier vorkommt."*

[79] See Erich von Holst, *Zur Verhaltensphysiologie bei Tieren und Menschen*, Gesammelte Abhandlungen, Vol. I, München, 1969, p. 239.

in the household of nature as the nutritive and sexual
instincts in the life process of the individual and the
species. But unlike these instincts, which are activated by
compelling bodily needs on one side, by outside stimulants
on the other, aggressive instincts in the animal kingdom
seem to be independent of such provocation; on the contrary, lack of provocation apparently leads to instinct
frustration, to "repressed" aggressiveness, which according
to psychologists causes a damming up of "energy" whose
eventual explosion will be all the more dangerous. (It is
as though the *sensation* of hunger in man would increase
with the decrease of hungry people.) [80] In this interpretation, violence without provocation is "natural"; if it has
lost its *rationale,* basically its function in self-preservation,
it becomes "irrational," and this is allegedly the reason
why men can be more "beastly" than other animals. (In the
literature we are constantly reminded of the generous behavior of wolves, who do not kill the defeated enemy.)

Quite apart from the misleading transposition of physical terms such as "energy" and "force" to biological and
zoological data, where they do not make sense because they
cannot be measured,[81] I fear there lurks behind these

---

[80] To counter the absurdity of this conclusion a distinction is made
between endogenous, spontaneous instincts, for instance, aggression,
and reactive drives such as hunger. But a distinction between spontaneity and reactivity makes no sense in a discussion of innate impulses. In the world of nature there is no spontaneity, properly
speaking, and instincts or drives only manifest the highly complex
way in which all living organisms, including man, are adapted to
its processes.

[81] The hypothetical character of Konrad Lorenz's *On Aggression*
(New York, 1966) is clarified in the interesting collection of essays
on aggression and adaptation edited by Alexander Mitscherlich
under the title *Bis hierher und nicht weiter. Ist die menschliche
Aggression unbefriedbar?*, München, 1968.

newest "discoveries" the oldest definition of the nature of man—the definition of man as the *animal rationale,* according to which we are distinct from other animal species in nothing but the additional attribute of reason. Modern science, starting uncritically from this old assumption, has gone far in "proving" that men share all other properties with some species of the animal kingdom—except that the additional gift of "reason" makes man a more dangerous beast. It is the use of reason that makes us dangerously "irrational," because this reason is the property of an "aboriginally instinctual being." [82] The scientists know, of course, that it is man the toolmaker who has invented those long-range weapons that free him from the "natural" restraints we find in the animal kingdom, and that tool-making is a highly complex *mental* activity.[83] Hence science is called upon to cure us of the side effects of reason by manipulating and controlling our instincts, usually by finding harmless outlets for them after their "life-promoting function" has disappeared. The standard of behavior is again derived from other animal species, in which the function of the life instincts has not been destroyed through the intervention of human reason. And the specific distinction between man and beast is now, strictly speaking, no longer reason (the *lumen naturale* of the human animal) but science, the knowledge of these stand-

---

[82] von Holst, *op. cit.,* p. 283: *"Nicht, weil wir Verstandeswesen, sondern weil wir ausserdem ganz urtümliche Triebwesen sind, ist unser Dasein im Zeitalter der Technik gefährdet."*

[83] Long-range weapons, seen by the polemologists as having freed man's aggressive instincts to the point where the controls safeguarding the species do not work any longer (see Tinbergen, *op. cit.*), are taken by Otto Klineberg ("Fears of a Psychologist," in Calder, *op. cit.,* p. 208) rather as an indication "that personal aggressiveness played [no] important role as a motive for war." Soldiers, one would like to continue the argument, are not killers, and killers—those with "personal aggressiveness"—are probably not even good soldiers.

ards and the techniques applying them. According to this view, man acts irrationally and like a beast if he refuses to listen to the scientists or is ignorant of their latest findings. As against these theories and their implications, I shall argue in what follows that violence is neither beastly nor irrational—whether we understand these terms in the ordinary language of the humanists or in accordance with scientific theories.

That violence often springs from rage is a commonplace, and rage can indeed be irrational and pathological, but so can every other human affect. It is no doubt possible to create conditions under which men are dehumanized—such as concentration camps, torture, famine—but this does not mean that they become animal-like; and under such conditions, not rage and violence, but their conspicuous absence is the clearest sign of dehumanization. Rage is by no means an automatic reaction to misery and suffering as such; no one reacts with rage to an incurable disease or to an earthquake or, for that matter, to social conditions that seem to be unchangeable. Only where there is reason to suspect that conditions could be changed and are not does rage arise. Only when our sense of justice is offended do we react with rage, and this reaction by no means necessarily reflects personal injury, as is demonstrated by the whole history of revolution, where invariably members of the upper classes touched off and then led the rebellions of the oppressed and downtrodden. To resort to violence when confronted with outrageous events or conditions is enormously tempting because of its inherent immediacy and swiftness. To act with *deliberate* speed goes against the grain of rage and violence, but this does not make them irrational. On the contrary, in private as well as public life there are situations in which the very swiftness of a violent act may be the only appropriate remedy. The point is not that this permits us to let off steam—

which indeed can be equally well done by pounding the table or slamming the door. The point is that under certain circumstances violence—acting without argument or speech and without counting the consequences—is the only way to set the scales of justice right again. (Billy Budd, striking dead the man who bore false witness against him, is the classical example.) In this sense, rage and the violence that sometimes—not always—goes with it belong among the "natural" *human* emotions, and to cure man of them would mean nothing less than to dehumanize or emasculate him. That such acts, in which men take the law into their own hands for justice's sake, are in conflict with the constitutions of civilized communities is undeniable; but their antipolitical character, so manifest in Melville's great story, does not mean that they are inhuman or "merely" emotional.

Absence of emotions neither causes nor promotes rationality. "Detachment and equanimity" in view of "unbearable tragedy" can indeed be "terrifying," [84] namely, when they are not the result of control but an evident manifestation of incomprehension. In order to respond reasonably one must first of all be "moved," and the opposite of emotional is not "rational," whatever that may mean, but either the inability to be moved, usually a pathological phenomenon, or sentimentality, which is a perversion of feeling. Rage and violence turn irrational only when they are directed against substitutes, and this, I am afraid, is precisely what the psychiatrists and polemologists concerned with human aggressiveness recommend, and what corresponds, alas, to certain moods and unreflecting attitudes in society at large. We all know, for example, that

[84] I am paraphrasing a sentence of Noam Chomsky (*op. cit.*, p. 371), who is very good in exposing the "façade of toughmindedness and pseudoscience" and the intellectual "vacuity" behind it, especially in the debates about the war in Vietnam.

it has become rather fashionable among white liberals to react to Negro grievances with the cry, "We are all guilty," and Black Power has proved only too happy to take advantage of this "confession" to instigate an irrational "black rage." Where all are guilty, no one is; confessions of collective guilt are the best possible safeguard against the discovery of culprits, and the very magnitude of the crime the best excuse for doing nothing. In this particular instance, it is, in addition, a dangerous and obfuscating escalation of racism into some higher, less tangible regions. The real rift between black and white is not healed by being translated into an even less reconcilable conflict between collective innocence and collective guilt. "All white men are guilty" is not only dangerous nonsense but also racism in reverse, and it serves quite effectively to give the very real grievances and rational emotions of the Negro population an outlet into irrationality, an escape from reality.

Moreover, if we inquire historically into the causes likely to transform *engagés* into *enragés,* it is not injustice that ranks first, but hypocrisy. Its momentous role in the later stages of the French Revolution, when Robespierre's war on hypocrisy transformed the "despotism of liberty" into the Reign of Terror, is too well known to be discussed here; but it is important to remember that this war had been declared long before by the French moralists who saw in hypocrisy the vice of all vices and found it ruling supreme in "good society," which somewhat later was called bourgeois society. Not many authors of rank glorified violence for violence's sake; but these few—Sorel, Pareto, Fanon—were motivated by a much deeper hatred of bourgeois society and were led to a much more radical break with its moral standards than the conventional Left, which was chiefly inspired by compassion and a burning desire for justice. To tear the mask of hypocrisy from the

face of the enemy, to unmask him and the devious machin-
ations and manipulations that permit him to rule without
using violent means, that is, to provoke action even at the
risk of annihilation so that the truth may come out—these
are still among the strongest motives in today's violence on
the campuses and in the streets.[85] And this violence again
is not irrational. Since men live in a world of appearances
and, in their dealing with it, depend on manifestation,
hypocrisy's conceits—as distinguished from expedient ruses,
followed by disclosure in due time—cannot be met by so-
called reasonable behavior. Words can be relied on only
if one is sure that their function is to reveal and not to
conceal. It is the semblance of rationality, much more than
the interests behind it, that provokes rage. To use reason
when reason is used as a trap is not "rational"; just as to
use a gun in self-defense is not "irrational." This violent
reaction against hypocrisy, however justifiable in its own
terms, loses its *raison d'être* when it tries to develop a
strategy of its own with specific goals; it becomes "irrational" the moment it is "rationalized," that is, the
moment the re-action in the course of a contest turns into
an action, and the hunt for suspects, accompanied by the
psychological hunt for ulterior motives, begins.[86]

Although the effectiveness of violence, as I remarked
before, does not depend on numbers—one machine gunner

[85] "If one reads the SDS publications one sees that they have frequently recommended provocations of the police as a strategy for
'unmasking' the violence of the authorities." Spender (*op. cit.*, p. 92)
comments that this kind of violence "leads to doubletalk in which
the provocateur is playing at one and the same time the role of
assailant and victim." The war on hypocrisy harbors a number of
great dangers, some of which I examined briefly in *On Revolution*,
New York, 1963, pp. 91-101.

[86] See appendix XV, p. 195.

can hold hundreds of well-organized people at bay—nonetheless in collective violence its most dangerously attractive features come to the fore, and this by no means because there is safety in numbers. It is perfectly true that in military as well as revolutionary action "individualism is the first [value] to disappear"; [87] in its stead, we find a kind of group coherence which is more intensely felt and proves to be a much stronger, though less lasting, bond than all the varieties of friendship, civil or private.[88] To be sure, in all illegal enterprises, criminal or political, the group, for the sake of its own safety, will require "that each individual perform an irrevocable action" in order to burn his bridges to respectable society before he is admitted into the community of violence. But once a man is admitted, he will fall under the intoxicating spell of "the practice of violence [which] binds men together as a whole, since each individual forms a violent link in the great chain, a part of the great organism of violence which has surged upward." [89]

Fanon's words point to the well-known phenomenon of brotherhood on the battlefield, where the noblest, most selfless deeds are often daily occurrences. Of all equalizers, death seems to be the most potent, at least in the few extraordinary situations where it is permitted to play a political role. Death, whether faced in actual dying or in the inner awareness of one's own mortality, is perhaps the most antipolitical experience there is. It signifies that we shall disappear from the world of appearances and shall leave the company of our fellow-men, which are the condi-

[87] Fanon, *op. cit.* p. 47.

[88] J. Glenn Gray, *The Warriors* (New York, 1959; now available in paperback), is most perceptive and instructive on this point. It should be read by everyone interested in the practice of violence.

[89] Fanon, *op. cit.*, pp. 85 and 93, respectively.

tions of all politics. As far as human experience is concerned, death indicates an extreme of loneliness and impotence. But faced collectively and in action, death changes its countenance; now nothing seems more likely to intensify our vitality than its proximity. Something we are usually hardly aware of, namely, that our own death is accompanied by the potential immortality of the group we belong to and, in the final analysis, of the species, moves into the center of our experience. It is as though life itself, the immortal life of the species, nourished, as it were, by the sempiternal dying of its individual members, is "surging upward," is actualized in the practice of violence.

It would be wrong, I think, to speak here of mere sentiments. After all, one of the outstanding properties of the human condition is here finding an adequate experience. In our context, however, the point of the matter is that these experiences, whose elementary force is beyond doubt, have never found an institutional, political expression, and that death as an equalizer plays hardly any role in political philosophy, although human mortality—the fact that men are "mortals," as the Greeks used to say—was understood as the strongest motive for political action in prephilosophic political thought. It was the certainty of death that made men seek immortal fame in deed and word and that prompted them to establish a body politic which was potentially immortal. Hence, politics was precisely a means by which to escape from the equality before death into a distinction assuring some measure of deathlessness. (Hobbes is the only political philosopher in whose work death, in the form of fear of violent death, plays a crucial role. But it is not equality before death that is decisive for Hobbes; it is the equality of fear resulting from the equal ability to kill possessed by everyone that persuades men in the state of nature to bind themselves into a commonwealth.) At any event, no body politic I know of was ever founded on equality before death and its actualization in violence; the suicide squads in history, which were indeed organized on this principle and therefore often called themselves "brotherhoods," can hardly be counted among political organizations. But it is true that the strong fraternal sentiments collective violence engenders have misled many good people into the hope that a new community together with a "new man" will arise out of it. The hope is an illusion for the simple reason that no human relationship is more transitory than this kind of brotherhood, which can be actualized only under conditions of immediate danger to life and limb.

That, however, is but one side of the matter. Fanon concludes his praise of the practice of violence by remarking that in this kind of struggle the people realize "that life is an unending contest," that violence is an element of life. And does that not sound plausible? Have not men always equated death with "eternal rest," and does it not follow that where we have life we have struggle and unrest? Is not quiet a clear manifestation of lifelessness or decay? Is not violent action a prerogative of the young—those who presumably are fully alive? Therefore are not praise of life and praise of violence the same? Sorel, at any rate, thought along these lines sixty years ago. Before Spengler, he predicted the "Decline of the Occident," having observed clear signs of abatement in the European class struggle. The bourgeoisie, he argued, had lost the "energy" to play its role in the class struggle; only if the proletariat could be persuaded to use violence in order to reaffirm class distinctions and awaken the fighting spirit of the bourgeoisie could Europe be saved.[90]

Hence, long before Konrad Lorenz discovered the life-

[90] Sorel, *op. cit.*, chapter 2, "On Violence and the Decadence of the Middle Classes."

promoting function of aggression in the animal kingdom, violence was praised as a manifestation of the life force and specifically of its creativity. Sorel, inspired by Bergson's *élan vital*, aimed at a philosophy of creativity designed for "producers" and polemically directed against the consumer society and its intellectuals; both groups, he felt, were parasites. The image of the bourgeois—peaceful, complacent, hypocritical, bent on pleasure, without will to power, a late product of capitalism rather than its representative—and the image of the intellectual, whose theories are "constructions" instead of "expressions of the will," [91] are hopefully counterbalanced in his work by the image of the worker. Sorel sees the worker as the "producer," who will create the new "moral qualities, which are necessary to improve production," destroy "the Parliaments [which] are as packed as shareholders' meetings," [92] and oppose to "the image of Progress . . . the image of total catastrophe," when "a kind of irresistible wave will pass over the old civilization." [93] The new values turn out to be not very new. They are a sense of honor, desire for fame and glory, the spirit of fighting without hatred and "without the spirit of revenge," and indifference to material advantages. Still, they are indeed the very virtues that were conspicuously absent from bourgeois society.[94] "Social war, by making an appeal to the honor which develops so naturally in all organized armies, can eliminate those evil feelings against which morality would remain

[91] *Ibidem*, "Introduction, Letter to Daniel Halevy," iv.

[92] *Ibidem*, chapter 7, "The Ethics of the Producers," I.

[93] *Ibidem*, chapter 4, "The Proletarian Strike," II.

[94] *Ibidem;* see especially chapter 5, III, and chapter 3, "Prejudices against Violence," III.

powerless. If this were the only reason . . . this reason alone would, it seems to me, be decisive in favor of the apologists for violence." [95]

Much can be learned from Sorel about the motives that prompt men to glorify violence in the abstract, and even more from his more gifted Italian contemporary, also of French formation, Vilfredo Pareto. Fanon, who had an infinitely greater intimacy with the practice of violence than either, was greatly influenced by Sorel and used his categories even when his own experiences spoke clearly against them.[96] The decisive experience that persuaded Sorel as well as Pareto to stress the factor of violence in revolutions was the Dreyfus Affair in France, when, in the words of Pareto, they were "amazed to see [the Dreyfusards] employing against their opponents the same vil-

---

[95] *Ibidem,* Appendix 2, "Apology for Violence."

[96] This has recently been stressed by Barbara Deming in her plea for nonviolent action—"On Revolution and Equilibrium," in *Revolution: Violent and Nonviolent,* reprinted from *Liberation,* February, 1968. She says about Fanon, on p. 3: "It is my conviction that he can be quoted as well to plead for nonviolence. . . . Every time you find the word 'violence' in his pages, substitute for it the phrase 'radical and uncompromising action.' I contend that with the exception of a very few passages this substitution can be made, and that the action he calls for could just as well be nonviolent action." Even more important for my purposes: Miss Deming also tries to distinguish clearly between power and violence, and she recognizes that "nonviolent disruption" means "to exert force. . . . It resorts even to what can only be called physical force" (p. 6). However, she curiously underestimates the effect of this force of disruption, which stops short only of physical injury, when she says, "the human rights of the adversary are respected" (p. 7). Only the opponent's right to life, but none of the other human rights, is actually respected. The same is of course true for those who advocate "violence against things" as opposed to "violence against persons."

lainous methods that they had themselves denounced." [97] At that juncture they discovered what we call today the Establishment and what earlier was called the System, and it was this discovery that made them turn to the praise of violent action and made Pareto, for his part, despair of the working class. (Pareto understood that the rapid integration of the workers into the social and political body of the nation actually amounted to "an alliance of bourgeoisie and working people," to the "embourgeoisement" of the workers, which then, according to him, gave rise to a new system, which he called "Pluto-democracy"—a mixed form of government, plutocracy being the bourgeois regime and democracy the regime of the workers.) The reason Sorel held on to his Marxist faith in the working class was that the workers were the "producers," the only creative element in society, those who, according to Marx, were bound to liberate the productive forces of mankind; the trouble was only that as soon as the workers had reached a satisfactory level of working and living conditions, they stubbornly refused to remain proletarians and play their revolutionary role.

Something else, however, which became fully manifest only in the decades after Sorel's and Pareto's death, was incomparably more disastrous to this view. The enormous growth of productivity in the modern world was by no means due to an increase in the workers' productivity, but exclusively the development of technology, and this depended neither on the working class nor on the bourgeoisie, but on the scientists. The "intellectuals," much despised by Sorel and Pareto, suddenly ceased to be a marginal social group and emerged as a new elite, whose

[97] Quoted from S. E. Finer's instructive essay "Pareto and Pluto-Democracy: The Retreat to Galapagos," in *The American Political Science Review*, June, 1968.

work, having changed the conditions of human life almost beyond recognition in a few decades, has remained essential for the functioning of society. There are many reasons why this new group has not, or not yet, developed into a power elite, but there is indeed every reason to believe with Daniel Bell that "not only the best talents, but eventually the entire complex of social prestige and social status, will be rooted in the intellectual and scientific communities." [98] Its members are more dispersed and less bound by clear interests than groups in the old class system; hence, they have no drive to organize themselves and lack experience in all matters pertaining to power. Also, being much more closely bound to cultural traditions, of which the revolutionary tradition is one, they cling with greater tenacity to categories of the past that prevent them from understanding the present and their own role in it. It is often touching to watch with what nostalgic sentiments the most rebellious of our students expect the "true" revolutionary impetus to come from those groups in society that denounce them the more vehemently the more they have to lose by anything that could disturb the smooth functioning of the consumer society. For better or worse—and I think there is every reason to be fearful as well as hopeful—the really new and potentially revolutionary class in society will consist of intellectuals, and their potential power, as yet unrealized, is very great, perhaps too great for the good of mankind.[99] But these are speculations.

However that may be, in this context we are chiefly interested in the strange revival of the life philosophies of Bergson and Nietzsche in their Sorelian version. We all

[98] "Notes on the Post-Industrial Society," *The Public Interest,* No. 6, 1967.

[99] See appendix XVI, p. 196.

know to what extent this old combination of violence, life, and creativity figures in the rebellious state of mind of the present generation. No doubt the emphasis on the sheer factuality of living, and hence on love-making as life's most glorious manifestation, is a response to the real possibility of constructing a doomsday machine and destroying all life on earth. But the categories in which the new glorifiers of life understand themselves are not new. To see the productivity of society in the image of life's "creativity" is at least as old as Marx, to believe in violence as a life-promoting force is at least as old as Nietzsche, and to think of creativity as man's highest good is at least as old as Bergson.

And this seemingly so novel biological justification of violence is again closely connected with the most pernicious elements in our oldest traditions of political thought. According to the traditional concept of power, equated, as we saw, with violence, power is expansionist by nature. It "has an inner urge to grow," it is creative because "the instinct of growth is proper to it." [100] Just as in the realm of organic life everything either grows or declines and dies, so in the realm of human affairs power supposedly can sustain itself only through expansion; otherwise it shrinks and dies. "That which stops growing begins to rot," goes a Russian saying from the entourage of Catherine the Great. Kings, we are told, were killed "not because of their tyranny but because of their weakness. The people erect scaffolds, not as the moral punishment of despotism, but as the *biological* penalty for weakness" (my italics). Revolutions, therefore, were directed against the established powers "only to the outward view." Their true "effect was to give Power a new vigour and poise, and to pull down the obstacles which had long obstructed its de-

---

[100] Jouvenel, *op. cit.*, pp. 114 and 123, respectively.

velopment." [101] When Fanon speaks of the "creative madness" present in violent action, he is still thinking in this tradition. [102]

Nothing, in my opinion, could be theoretically more dangerous than the tradition of organic thought in political matters by which power and violence are interpreted in biological terms. As these terms are understood today, life and life's alleged creativity are their common denominator, so that violence is justified on the ground of creativity. The organic metaphors with which our entire present discussion of these matters, especially of the riots, is permeated —the notion of a "sick society," of which riots are symptoms, as fever is a symptom of disease—can only promote violence in the end. Thus the debate between those who propose violent means to restore "law and order" and those who propose nonviolent reforms begins to sound ominously like a discussion between two physicians who debate the relative advantages of surgical as opposed to medical treatment of their patient. The sicker the patient is supposed to be, the more likely that the surgeon will have the last word. Moreover, so long as we talk in nonpolitical, biological terms, the glorifiers of violence can appeal to the undeniable fact that in the household of nature destruction and creation are but two sides of the natural process, so that collective violent action, quite apart from its inherent attraction, may appear as natural a prerequisite for the collective life of mankind as the struggle for survival and violent death for continuing life in the animal kingdom.

The danger of being carried away by the deceptive plausibility of organic metaphors is particularly great where the racial issue is involved. Racism, white or black,

[101] *Ibidem*, pp. 187 and 188.

[102] Fanon, *op. cit.*, p. 95.

is fraught with violence by definition because it objects to natural organic facts—a white or black skin—which no persuasion or power could change; all one can do, when the chips are down, is to exterminate their bearers. Racism, as distinguished from race, is not a fact of life, but an ideology, and the deeds it leads to are not reflex actions, but deliberate acts based on pseudo-scientific theories. Violence in interracial struggle is always murderous, but it is not "irrational"; it is the logical and rational consequence of racism, by which I do not mean some rather vague prejudices on either side, but an explicit ideological system. Under the pressure of power, prejudices, as distinguished from both interests and ideologies, may yield—as we saw happen with the highly successful civil-rights movement, which was entirely nonviolent. ("By 1964 . . . most Americans were convinced that subordination and, to a lesser degree, segregation were wrong.") [103] But while boycotts, sit-ins, and demonstrations were successful in eliminating discriminatory laws and ordinances in the South, they proved utter failures and became counterproductive when they encountered the social conditions in the large urban centers—the stark needs of the black ghettos on one side, the overriding interests of white lower-income groups in respect to housing and education on the other. All this mode of action could do, and indeed did, was to bring these conditions into the open, into the street, where the basic irreconcilability of interests was dangerously exposed.

But even today's violence, black riots, and the potential violence of the white backlash are not yet manifestations of racist ideologies and their murderous logic. (The riots,

[103] Robert M. Fogelson, "Violence as Protest," in *Urban Riots: Violence and Social Change,* Proceedings of the Academy of Political Science, Columbia University, 1968.

as has recently been stated, are "articulate protests against genuine grievances";[104] indeed "restraint and selectivity— or . . . rationality are certainly among [their] most crucial features." [105] And much the same is true for the backlash phenomena, which, contrary to all predictions, have not been characterized by violence up to now. It is the perfectly rational reaction of certain interest groups which furiously protest against being singled out to pay the full price for ill-designed integration policies whose consequences their authors can easily escape.) [106] The greatest danger comes from the other direction; since violence always needs justification, an escalation of the violence in the streets may bring about a truly racist ideology to justify it. Black racism, so blatantly evident in James Forman's "Manifesto" is probably more a reaction to the chaotic rioting of the last years than its cause. It could, of course, provoke a really violent white backlash, whose greatest danger would be the transformation of white prejudices into a full-fledged racist ideology for which "law and order" would indeed become a mere façade. In this still unlikely case, the climate of opinion in the country might deteriorate to the point where a majority of its citizens would be willing to pay the price of the invisible terror of a police state for law and order in the streets. What we have now, a kind of police backlash, quite brutal and highly visible, is nothing of the sort.

Behavior and arguments in interest conflicts are not notorious for their "rationality." Nothing, unfortunately, has so constantly been refuted by reality as the credo of "enlightened self-interest," in its literal version as well as

[104] *Ibidem.*

[105] *Ibidem.* See also the excellent article "Official Interpretation of Racial Riots" by Allan A. Silver in the same collection.

[106] See appendix XVII, p. 197.

in its more sophisticated Marxian variant. Some experience plus a little reflection teach, on the contrary, that it goes against the very nature of self-interest to be enlightened. To take as an example from everyday life the current interest conflict between tenant and landlord: enlightened interest would focus on a building fit for human habitation, but this interest is quite different from, and in most cases opposed to, the landlord's self-interest in high profit and the tenant's in low rent. The common answer of an arbiter, supposedly the spokesman of "enlightenment," namely, that *in the long run* the interest of the building is the *true* interest of both landlord and tenant, leaves out of account the time factor, which is of paramount importance for all concerned. Self-interest is interested in the self, and the self dies or moves out or sells the house; because of its changing condition, that is, ultimately because of the human condition of mortality, the self *qua* self cannot reckon in terms of long-range interest, i.e. the interest of a world that survives its inhabitants. Deterioration of the building is a matter of years; a rent increase or a temporarily lower profit rate are for today or for tomorrow. And something similar, *mutatis mutandis,* is of course true for labor-management conflicts and the like. Self-interest, when asked to yield to "true" interest—that is, the interest of the world as distinguished from that of the self—will always reply, Near is my shirt, but nearer is my skin. That may not be particularly reasonable, but it is quite realistic; it is the not very noble but adequate response to the time discrepancy between men's private lives and the altogether different life expectancy of the public world. To expect people, who have not the slightest notion of what the *res publica,* the public thing, is, to behave nonviolently and argue rationally in matters of interest is neither realistic nor reasonable.

Violence, being instrumental by nature, is rational to the extent that it is effective in reaching the end that must justify it. And since when we act we never know with any certainty the eventual consequences of what we are doing, violence can remain rational only if it pursues short-term goals. Violence does not promote causes, neither history nor revolution, neither progress nor reaction; but it can serve to dramatize grievances and bring them to public attention. As Conor Cruise O'Brien (in a debate on the legitimacy of violence in the Theatre of Ideas) once remarked, quoting William O'Brien, the nineteenth-century Irish agrarian and nationalist agitator: Sometimes "violence is the only way of ensuring a hearing for moderation." To ask the impossible in order to obtain the possible is not always counterproductive. And indeed, violence, contrary to what its prophets try to tell us, is more the weapon of reform than of revolution. France would not have received the most radical bill since Napoleon to change its antiquated education system if the French students had not rioted; if it had not been for the riots of the spring term, no one at Columbia University would have dreamed of accepting reforms; [107] and it is probably quite true that in West Germany the existence of "dissenting minorities is not even noticed unless they engage in provocation." [108] No doubt, "violence pays," but

[107] "At Columbia, before last year's uprising, for example, a report on student life and another on faculty housing had been gathering dust in the president's office," as Fred Hechinger reported in the New York *Times*, "The Week in Review" of May 4, 1969.

[108] Rudi Dutschke, as quoted in *Der Spiegel*, February 10, 1969, p. 27. Günter Grass, speaking in much the same vein after the attack on Dutschke in spring 1968, also stresses the relation between reforms and violence: "The youth protest movement has brought the fragility of our insufficiently established democracy into evidence.

the trouble is that it pays indiscriminately, for "soul courses" and instruction in Swahili as well as for real reforms. And since the tactics of violence and disruption make sense only for short-term goals, it is even more likely, as was recently the case in the United States, that the established power will yield to nonsensical and obviously damaging demands—such as admitting students without the necessary qualifications and instructing them in non-existent subjects—if only such "reforms" can be made with comparative ease, than that violence will be effective with respect to the relatively long-term objective of structural change.[109] Moreover, the danger of violence, even if it moves consciously within a nonextremist framework of short-term goals, will always be that the means overwhelm the end. If goals are not achieved rapidly, the result will be not merely defeat but the introduction of the practice of violence into the whole body politic. Action is irreversible, and a return to the *status quo* in case of defeat is always unlikely. The practice of violence, like all action, changes the world, but the most probable change is to a more violent world.

In this it has been successful, but it is far from certain where this success will lead; either it will bring about long-overdue reforms . . . or . . . the uncertainty that has now been laid bare will provide false prophets with promising markets and free advertising." See "Violence Rehabilitated," in *Speak Out!*, New York, 1969.

[109] Another question, which we cannot discuss here, is to what an extent the whole university system is still capable of reforming itself. I think there is no general answer. Even though the student rebellion is a global phenomenon, the university systems themselves are by no means uniform and vary not only from country to country but often from institution to institution; all solutions of the problem must spring from, and correspond to, strictly local conditions. Thus, in some countries the university crisis may even broaden into a government crisis—as *Der Spiegel* (June 23, 1969) thought possible in discussing the German situation.

Finally—to come back to Sorel's and Pareto's earlier denunciation of the system as such—the greater the bureaucratization of public life, the greater will be the attraction of violence. In a fully developed bureaucracy there is nobody left with whom one can argue, to whom one can present grievances, on whom the pressures of power can be exerted. Bureaucracy is the form of government in which everybody is deprived of political freedom, of the power to act; for the rule by Nobody is not no-rule, and where all are equally powerless we have a tyranny without a tyrant. The crucial feature in the student rebellions around the world is that they are directed everywhere against the ruling bureaucracy. This explains what at first glance seems so disturbing—that the rebellions in the East demand precisely those freedoms of speech and thought that the young rebels in the West say they despise as irrelevant. On the level of ideologies, the whole thing is confusing; it is much less so if we start from the obvious fact that the huge party machines have succeeded everywhere in overruling the voice of the citizens, even in countries where freedom of speech and association is still intact. The dissenters and resisters in the East demand free speech and thought as the preliminary conditions for political action; the rebels in the West live under conditions where these preliminaries no longer open the channels for action, for the meaningful exercise of freedom. What matters to them is, indeed, *"Praxisentzug,"* the suspension of action, as Jens Litten, a German student, has aptly called it.[110] The transformation of government into administration, or of republics into bureaucracies, and the disastrous shrinkage of the public realm that went with it have a long and complicated history throughout the modern age; and this process has been considerably

[110] See appendix XVIII, p. 198.

accelerated during the last hundred years through the rise of party bureaucracies. (Seventy years ago Pareto recognized that "freedom . . . by which I mean the power to act shrinks every day, save for criminals, in the so-called free and democratic countries.")[111] What makes man a political being is his faculty of action; it enables him to get together with his peers, to act in concert, and to reach out for goals and enterprises that would never enter his mind, let alone the desires of his heart, had he not been given this gift—to embark on something new. Philosophically speaking, to act is the human answer to the condition of natality. Since we all come into the world by virtue of birth, as newcomers and beginnings, we are able to start something new; without the fact of birth we would not even know what novelty is, all "action" would be either mere behavior or preservation. No other faculty except language, neither reason nor consciousness, distinguishes us so radically from all animal species. To act and to begin are not the same, but they are closely interconnected.

None of the properties of creativity is adequately expressed in metaphors drawn from the life process. To beget and to give birth are no more creative than to die is annihilating; they are but different phases of the same, ever-recurring cycle in which all living things are held as though they were spellbound. Neither violence nor power is a natural phenomenon, that is, a manifestation of the life process; they belong to the political realm of human affairs whose essentially human quality is guaranteed by man's faculty of action, the ability to begin something new. And I think it can be shown that no other human ability has suffered to such an extent from the progress of the modern age, for progress, as we have come to understand it, means growth, the relentless process of more and

---

[111] Pareto, quoted from Finer, *op. cit.*

more, of bigger and bigger. The bigger a country becomes in terms of population, of objects, and of possessions, the greater will be the need for administration and with it the anonymous power of the administrators. Pavel Kohout, a Czech author, writing in the heyday of the Czechoslovakian experiment with freedom, defined a "free citizen" as a "Citizen-Co-ruler." He meant nothing more or less than the "participatory democracy" of which we have heard so much in recent years in the West. Kohout added that what the world today stands in greatest need of may well be "a new example" if "the next thousand years are not to become an era of supercivilized monkeys"—or, even worse, of "man turned into a chicken or a rat," ruled over by an "elite" that derives its power "from the wise counsels of . . . intellectual aides" who actually believe that men in think tanks are thinkers and that computers can think; "the counsels may turn out to be incredibly insidious and, instead of pursuing human objectives, may pursue completely abstract problems that had been transformed in an unforeseen manner in the artificial brain." [112]

This new example will hardly be set by the practice of violence, although I am inclined to think that much of the present glorification of violence is caused by severe frustration of the faculty of action in the modern world. It is simply true that riots in the ghettos and rebellions on the campuses make "people feel they are acting together in a way that they rarely can." [113] We do not know if these occurrences are the beginnings of something new—the "new example"—or the death pangs of a faculty that

[112] See Günter Grass and Pavel Kohout, *Briefe über die Grenze*, Hamburg, 1968, pp. 88 and 90, respectively; and Andrei D. Sakharov, *op. cit.*

[113] Herbert J. Gans, "The Ghetto Rebellions and Urban Class Conflict," in *Urban Riots*, *op. cit.*

mankind is about to lose. As things stand today, when we see how the superpowers are bogged down under the monstrous weight of their own bigness, it looks as though the setting of a "new example" will have a chance, if at all, in a small country, or in small, well-defined sectors in the mass societies of the large powers.

The disintegration processes which have become so manifest in recent years—the decay of public services: schools, police, mail delivery, garbage collection, transportation, et cetera; the death rate on the highways and the traffic problems in the cities; the pollution of air and water—are the automatic results of the needs of mass societies that have become unmanageable. They are accompanied and often accelerated by the simultaneous decline of the various party systems, all of more or less recent origin and designed to serve the political needs of mass populations—in the West to make representative government possible when direct democracy would not do any longer because "the room will not hold all" (John Selden), and in the East to make absolute rule over vast territories more effective. Bigness is afflicted with vulnerability; cracks in the power structure of all but the small countries are opening and widening. And while no one can say with assurance where and when the breaking point has been reached, we can observe, almost measure, how strength and resiliency are insidiously destroyed, leaking, as it were, drop by drop from our institutions.

Moreover, there is the recent rise of a curious new brand of nationalism, usually understood as a swing to the Right, but more probably an indication of a growing, world-wide resentment against "bigness" as such. While national feelings formerly tended to unite various ethnic groups by focusing their political sentiments on the nation as a whole, we now watch how an ethnic "nationalism" begins to threaten with dissolution the oldest and best-established nation-states. The Scots and the Welsh, the Bretons and the Provençals, ethnic groups whose successful assimilation had been the prerequisite for the rise of the nation-state and had seemed completely assured, are turning to separatism in rebellion against the centralized governments in London and Paris. And just when centralization, under the impact of bigness, turned out to be counterproductive in its own terms, this country, founded, according to the federal principle, on the division of powers and powerful so long as this division was respected, threw itself headlong, to the unanimous applause of all "progressive" forces, into the new, for America, experiment of centralized administration—the federal government overpowering state powers and executive power eroding congressional powers.[114] It is as though this most successful European colony wished to share the fate of the mother countries in their decline, repeating in great haste the very errors the framers of the Constitution had set out to correct and to eliminate.

Whatever the administrative advantages and disadvantages of centralization may be, its political result is always the same: monopolization of power causes the drying up or oozing away of all authentic power sources in the country. In the United States, based on a great plurality of powers and their mutual checks and balances, we are confronted not merely with the disintegration of power structures, but with power, seemingly still intact and free to manifest itself, losing its grip and becoming ineffective. To speak of the impotence of power is no longer a witty paradox. Senator Eugene McCarthy's crusade in 1968 "to test the system" brought popular resentment against imperialist adventures into the open, provided the link between the opposition in the Senate and

114 See the important article of Henry Steele Commager, footnote 74.

that in the streets, enforced an at least temporary spectacular change in policy, and demonstrated how quickly the majority of the young rebels could become dealienated, jumping at this first opportunity not to abolish the system but to make it work again. And still, all this power could be crushed by the party bureaucracy, which, contrary to all traditions, preferred to lose the presidential election with an unpopular candidate who happened to be an *apparatchik*. (Something similar happened when Rockefeller lost the nomination to Nixon during the Republican convention.)

There are other examples to demonstrate the curious contradictions inherent in impotence of power. Because of the enormous effectiveness of teamwork in the sciences, which is perhaps the outstanding American contribution to modern science, we can control the most complicated processes with a precision that makes trips to the moon less dangerous than ordinary weekend excursions; but the allegedly "greatest power on earth" is helpless to end a war, clearly disastrous for all concerned, in one of the earth's smallest countries. It is as though we have fallen under a fairyland spell which permits us to do the "impossible" on the condition that we lose the capacity of doing the possible, to achieve fantastically extraordinary feats on the condition of no longer being able to attend properly to our everyday needs. If power has anything to do with the we-*will*-and-we-can, as distinguished from the mere we-can, then we have to admit that our power has become impotent. The progresses made by science have nothing to do with the I-will; they follow their own inexorable laws, compelling us to do whatever we can, regardless of consequences. Have the I-will and the I-can parted company? Was Valéry right when he said fifty years ago: *"On peut dire que tout ce que nous savons, c'est-à-dire tout ce que nous pouvons, a fini par s'opposer à ce que nous sommes"*? ("One can say that all we know, that is, all we have the power to do, has finally turned against what we are.")

Again, we do not know where these developments will lead us, but we know, or should know, that every decrease in power is an open invitation to violence—if only because those who hold power and feel it slipping from their hands, be they the government or be they the governed, have always found it difficult to resist the temptation to substitute violence for it.

Appendices

I, TO PAGE 115, NOTE 16

Professor B. C. Parekh, of Hull University, England, kindly drew my attention to the following passage in the section on Feuerbach from Marx's and Engels' *German Ideology* (1846), of which Engels later wrote: "The portion finished . . . only proves how incomplete at that time was our knowledge of economic history." "Both for the production on a mass scale of this communist consciousness, and for the success of the cause itself, the alteration of man [des Menschen] on a mass scale is necessary, an alteration which can only take place in a practical movement, a *revolution;* this revolution is necessary, therefore, not only because the ruling class cannot be overthrown in any other way, but also because the class *overthrowing* it can only in a revolution succeed in ridding itself of all the muck of ages and become fitted to found society anew." (Quoted from the edition by R. Pascal, New York, 1960, pp. xv and 69.) Even in these, as it were, pre-Marxist utterances, the distinction between Marx's and Sartre's positions is evident. Marx speaks of "the alteration of man on a mass scale," and of a "mass production of consciousness," not of the liberation of an individual through an isolated act of violence. (For the German text, see Marx/Engels *Gesamtausgabe,* 1932, I. Abteilung, vol. 5, pp. 59 f.)

II, TO PAGE 115, NOTE 17

The New Left's unconscious drifting away from Marxism has been duly noticed. See especially recent comments on the student movement by Leonard Schapiro in the *New York Review of Books* (December 5, 1968) and by Raymond Aron in *La Révolution Introuvable,* Paris, 1968. Both consider the new emphasis on violence to be a kind of backsliding either to pre-Marxian utopian socialism (Aron) or to the Russian anarchism of Nechaev and Bakunin (Schapiro), who "had much to say about the importance of violence as a factor of unity, as the binding force in a society or group, a century before the same ideas emerged in the works of Jean-Paul Sartre and Frantz Fanon." Aron writes in the same vein: *"Les chantres de la révolution de mai croient dépasser le marxisme . . . ils oublient un siècle d'histoire"* (p. 14). To a non-Marxist such a reversion would of course hardly be an argument; but for Sartre, who, for instance, writes *"Un prétendu 'dépassement' du marxisme ne sera au pis qu'un retour au prémarxisme, au mieux que la redécouverte d'une pensée déjà contenue dans la philosophie qu'on a cru dépasser"* ("Question de Méthode" in *Critique de la raison dialectique*, Paris, 1960, p. 17), it must constitute a formidable objection. (That Sartre and Aron, though political opponents, are in full agreement on this point is noteworthy. It shows to what an extent Hegel's concept of history dominates the thought of Marxists and non-Marxists alike.)

Sartre himself, in his *Critique of Dialectical Reason*, gives a kind of Hegelian explanation for his espousal of violence. His point of departure is that "need and scarcity determined the Manicheistic basis of action and morals" in present history, "whose truth is based on scarcity [and] must manifest itself in an antagonistic reciprocity between classes." Aggression is the consequence of need in a world where "there is not enough for all." Under such circumstances, violence is no longer a marginal phenomenon. "Violence and counter-violence are perhaps contingencies, but they are contingent necessities, and the imperative consequence of any attempt to destroy this inhumanity is that in destroying in the adversary the inhumanity of the contraman, I can only destroy in him the humanity of man, and realize in me his inhumanity. Whether I kill, torture, enslave . . . my aim is to suppress his freedom—it is an alien force, *de trop*." His model for a condition in which "each one is one too many . . . Each is *redundant* for the other" is a bus queue, the members of which obviously "take no notice of each other except as a number in a quantitative series." He concludes, "They reciprocally deny any link between each of their inner worlds." From this, it follows that praxis "is the negation of alterity, which is itself a negation"—a highly welcome conclusion, since the negation of a negation is an affirmation.

The flaw in the argument seems to me obvious. There is all the difference in the world between "not taking notice" and "denying," between "denying any link" with somebody and "negating" his otherness; and for a sane person there is still a considerable distance to travel from this theoretical "negation" to killing, torturing, and enslaving.

186

Most of the above quotations are drawn from R. D. Laing and D. G. Cooper, *Reason and Violence. A Decade of Sartre's Philosophy, 1950-1960*, London, 1964, Part Three. This seems legitimate because Sartre in his foreword says: *"J'ai lu attentivement l'ouvrage que vous avez bien voulu me confier et j'ai eu le grand plaisir d'y trouver un exposé très clair et très fidèle de ma pensée."*

III, TO PAGE 117, NOTE 20

They are indeed a mixed lot. Radical students congregate easily with dropouts, hippies, drug addicts, and psychopaths. The situation is further complicated by the insensitivity of the established powers to the often subtle distinctions between crime and irregularity, distinctions that are of great importance. Sit-ins and occupations of buildings are not the same as arson or armed revolt, and the difference is not just one of degree. (Contrary to the opinion of one member of Harvard's Board of Trustees, the occupation of a university building by students is not the same thing as the invasion of a branch of the First National City Bank by a street mob, for the simple reason that the students trespass upon a property whose use, to be sure, is subject to rules, but to which they belong and which belongs to them as much as to faculty and administration.) Even more alarming is the inclination of faculty as well as administration to treat drug addicts and criminal elements (in City College in New York and in Cornell University) with considerably more leniency than the authentic rebels.

Helmut Schelsky, the German social scientist, described as early as 1961 (in *Der Mensch in der wissenschaftlichen Zivilisation*, Köln und Opladen, 1961) the possibility of a "metaphysical nihilism," by which he meant the radical social and spiritual denial of "the whole process of man's scientific-technical reproduction," that is, the no said to "the rising world of a scientific civilization." To call this attitude "nihilistic" presupposes an acceptance of the modern world as the only possible world. The challenge of the young rebels concerns precisely this point. There is indeed much sense in turning the tables and stating, as Sheldon Wolin and John Schaar have done in *op. cit.*: "The great danger at present is that the established and the respectable . . . seem prepared to follow the most profoundly nihilistic denial possible, which is the denial of the future through denial of their own children, the bearers of the future."

Nathan Glazer, in an article, "Student Power at Berkeley," in *The Public Interest*'s special issue *The Universities*, Fall, 1968, writes: "The student radicals . . . remind me more of the Luddite machine smashers than the Socialist trade unionists who achieved citizenship and power for workers," and he concludes from this impression that Zbigniew Brzezinski (in an article about Columbia in *The New Republic*, June 1, 1968) may have been right in his diagnosis: "Very frequently revolutions are the last spasms of the past, and thus are not really revolutions but counter-revolutions, operating in the name of revolutions." Is not this bias in favor of marching forward at any price rather odd in two authors who are generally considered to be conservatives? And is it not even odder that Glazer should remain unaware of the decisive differences between manufacturing machinery in early nineteenth-century England and the hardware developed in the middle of the twentieth century which has turned out to be destructive even when it appeared to be most beneficial—the discovery of nuclear energy, automation, medicine whose healing powers have led to overpopulation, which in its turn will almost certainly lead to mass starvation, air pollution, et cetera?

IV, TO PAGE 118, NOTE 23

To look for precedents and analogies where there are none, to avoid reporting and reflecting on what is being done and what is being said in terms of the events themselves, under the pretext that we ought to learn the lessons of the past, particularly of the era between the two world wars, has become characteristic of a great many current discussions. Entirely free of this form of escapism is Stephen Spender's splendid and wise report on the student movement, quoted above. He is among the few of his generation to be fully alive to the present *and* to remember his own youth well enough to be aware of the differences in mood, style, thought, and action. ("Today's students are entirely different from the Oxbridge, Harvard, Princeton or Heidelberg students forty years back," p. 165.) But Spender's attitude is shared by all those, in no matter which generation, who are truly concerned with the world's and man's future as distinguished from those who play games with it. (Wolin and Schaar, *op. cit.*, speak of "the revival of a sense of shared destiny" as a bridge between the generations, of "our common fears that scientific weapons may destroy all life, that technology will increasingly disfigure men who live in the city, just as it has already debased the earth and obscured the sky"; that "the 'progress' of industry will destroy the possibility of interesting work; and that 'communications' will obliterate the last traces of the varied cultures which have been the inheritance of all but the most benighted societies.") It seems only natural that this should be true more frequently of physicists and biologists than of members of the social sciences, even though the students of the former faculties were much slower to rise in rebellion than their fellow classmates in the humanities. Thus Adolf Portmann, the famous Swiss biologist, sees the gap between the generations as having little if anything to do with a conflict between Young and Old; it coincides with the rise of nuclear science; "the resulting world situation is entirely new. . . . [It] cannot be compared to even the most powerful revolution of the past." (In a pamphlet entitled *Manipulation des Menschen als Schicksal und Bedrohung*, Zürich, 1969.) And Nobel Prize winner George Wald, of Harvard, in his famous speech at M.I.T. on March 4, 1969, rightly stressed that such teachers understand "the reasons of [their students'] uneasiness even better than they do," and, what is more, that they "share it," *op. cit.*

V, TO PAGE 119, NOTE 25

The present politicization of the universities, rightly deplored, is usually blamed on the rebellious students, who are accused of attacking the universities because they constitute the weakest link in the chain of established power. It is perfectly true that the universities will not be able to survive if "intellectual detachment and the disinterested search for truth" should come to an end; and, what is worse, it is unlikely that civilized society of any kind will be able to survive the disappearance of these curious institutions whose main social and political function lies precisely in their impartiality and independence from social pressure and political power. Power and truth, both perfectly legitimate in their own rights, are essentially distinct phenomena and their pursuit results in existentially different ways of life. Zbigniew Brzezinski, in "America in the Technotronic Age" (*Encounter*, January, 1968), sees this danger but is either resigned or at least not unduly alarmed by the prospect. Technotronics, he believes, will usher in a new " 'superculture' " under the guidance of the new "organization-oriented, application-minded intellectuals." (See especially Noam Chomsky's recent critical analysis "Objectivity and Liberal Scholarship" in *op. cit.*) Well, it is much more likely that this new breed of intellectuals, formerly known as technocrats, will usher in an age of tyranny and utter sterility.

However that may be, the point is that the politicization of the universities by the students' movement was preceded by the politicization of the universities by the established powers. The facts are too well known to need emphasizing, but it is good to keep in mind that this is not merely a matter of military research. Henry Steele Commager recently denounced "the University as Employment Agency" (*The New Republic*, February 24, 1968). Indeed, "by no stretch of the imagination can it be alleged that Dow Chemical Company, the Marines or the CIA are educational enterprises," or institutions whose goal is a search for truth. And Mayor John Lindsay raised the question of the university's right to call "itself a special institution, divorced from worldly pursuits, while it engages in real-estate speculation and helps plan and evaluate projects for the military in Vietnam" (New York *Times*, "The Week in Review," May 4, 1969). To pretend that the university is "the brain of society" or of the power structure is dangerous, arrogant nonsense —if only because society is not a "body," let alone a brainless one.

In order to avoid misunderstandings: I quite agree with Stephen Spender that it would be folly for the students to wreck the universities (although they are the only ones who could do so effectively for the simple reason that they have numbers, and therefore real power, on their side), since the campuses constitute not only their real, but also their only possible basis. "Without the university, there would be no students" (p. 22). But the universities will remain a basis for the students only so long as they provide the only place in society where power does not have the last word—all perversions and hypocrisies to the contrary notwithstanding. In the present situation, there is a danger that either students or, as in the case of Berkeley, the powers-that-be will run amuck; if this should happen, the young rebels would have simply spun one more thread into what has been aptly called "the pattern of disaster." (Professor Richard A. Falk, of Princeton.)

VI, TO PAGE 121, NOTE 30

Fred M. Hechinger, in an article, "Campus Crisis," in the New York *Times*, "The Week in Review" (May 4, 1969), writes: "Since the demands of the black students especially are usually justified in substance . . . the reaction is generally sympathetic." It seems characteristic of present attitudes in these matters that James Forman's "Manifesto to the White Christian Churches and the Jewish Synagogues in the United States and all other Racist Institutions," though publicly read and distributed, hence certainly "news that's fit to print," remained unpublished until the *New York Review of Books* (July 10, 1969) printed it without the Introduction. Its content, to be sure, is half-illiterate fantasy, and may not be meant seriously. But it is more than a joke, and that the Negro community moodily indulges today in such fantasies is no secret. That the authorities should be frightened is understandable. What can neither be understood nor condoned is their lack of imagination. Is it not obvious that Mr. Forman and his followers, if they find no opposition in the community at large and even are given a little appeasement money, will be forced to try to execute a program which they themselves perhaps never believed in?

VII, TO PAGE 121, NOTE 31

In a letter to the New York *Times* (dated April 9, 1969), Lynd mentions only "nonviolent disruptive actions such as strikes and sit-ins," ignoring for his purposes the tumultuous violent riots of the working class in the twenties, and raises the question why these tactics "accepted for a generation in labor-management relations . . . are rejected when practiced on a campus? . . . when a union organizer is fired from a factory bench, his associates walk off the job until the grievance is settled." It looks as though Lynd has accepted a university image, unfortunately not unfrequent among trustees and administrators, according to which the campus is owned by the board of trustees, which hires the administration to manage their property, which in turn hires the faculty as employees to serve its customers, the students. There is no reality that corresponds to this "image." No matter how sharp the conflicts may become in the academic world, they are not matters of clashing interests and class warfare.

VIII, TO PAGE 121, NOTE 32

Bayard Rustin, the Negro civil-rights leader, has said all that needed to be said on the matter: College officials should "stop capitulating to the stupid demands of Negro students"; it is wrong if one group's "sense of guilt and masochism permits another segment of society to hold guns in the name of justice"; black students were "suffering from the shock of integration" and looking for "an easy way out of their problems"; what Negro students need is "remedial training" so that they "can do mathematics and write a correct sentence," not "soul courses." (Quoted from the *Daily News*, April 28, 1969.) What a reflection on the moral and intellectual state of society that much courage was required to talk common sense in these matters! Even more frightening is the all too likely prospect that, in about five or ten years, this "education" in Swahili (a nineteenth-century kind of no-language spoken by the Arab ivory and slave caravans, a hybrid mixture of a Bantu dialect with an enormous vocabulary of Arab borrowings; see the Encyclopaedia Britannica, 1961), African literature, and other nonexistent subjects will be interpreted as another trap of the white man to prevent Negroes from acquiring an adequate education.

IX, TO PAGE 123, NOTE 36

James Forman's "Manifesto" (adopted by the National Black Economic Development Conference), which I mentioned before and which he presented to the Churches and Synagogues as "only a beginning of the reparations due us as people who have been exploited and degraded, brutalized, killed and persecuted," reads like a classical example of such futile dreams. According to him, "it follows from the laws of revolution that the most oppressed will make the revolution," whose ultimate goal is that "we must assume leadership, total control . . . inside of the United States of everything that exists. The time has passed when we are second in command and the white boy stands on top." In order to achieve this reversal, it will be necessary "to use whatever means necessary, including the use of force and power of the gun to bring down the colonizer." And while he, in the name of the community (which, of course, stands by no means behind him), "declares war," refuses to "share power with whites," and demands that "white people in this country . . . be willing to accept black leadership," he calls at the same time "upon all Christians and Jews to practice patience, tolerance, understanding and nonviolence" during the period it may still take— "whether it happens in a thousand years is of no consequence"—to seize power.

X, TO PAGE 126, NOTE 40

Jürgen Habermas, one of the most thoughtful and intelligent social scientists in Germany, is a good example of the difficulties these Marxists or former Marxists find in parting with any piece of the work of the master. In his recent *Technik und Wissenschaft als 'Ideologie'* (Frankfurt, 1968), he mentions several times that certain "key categories of Marx's theory, namely, class-struggle and ideology, can no longer be applied without ado (*umstandslos*)." A comparison with the essay of Andrei D. Sakharov quoted above shows how much easier it is for those who look on "capitalism" from the perspective of the disastrous Eastern experiments to discard outworn theories and slogans.

The sanctions of the laws, which, however, are not their essence, are directed against those citizens who—without withholding their support—wish to make an exception for themselves; the thief still expects the government to protect his newly acquired property. It has been noted that in the earliest legal systems there were no sanctions whatsoever. (See Jouvenel, *op. cit.*, p. 276.) The lawbreaker's punishment was banishment or outlawry; by breaking the law, the criminal had put himself outside the community constituted by it.

Passerin d'Entrèves (*op. cit.*, pp. 128 ff.), taking into account "the complexity of law, even of State law," has pointed out that "there are indeed laws which are 'directives' rather than 'imperatives', which are 'accepted' rather than 'imposed', and whose 'sanctions' do not necessarily consist in the possible use of force on the part of a 'sovereign'." Such laws, he has likened to "the rules of a game, or those of my club, or to those of the Church." I conform "because for me, unlike others of my fellow citizens, these rules are 'valid' rules."

I think Passerin d'Entrèves's comparison of the law with the "valid rules of the game" can be driven further. For the point of these rules is not that I submit to them voluntarily or recognize theoretically their validity, but that in practice I cannot enter the game unless I conform; my motive for acceptance is my wish to play, and since men exist only in the plural, my wish to play is identical with my wish to live. Every man is born into a community with pre-existing laws which he "obeys" first of all because there is no other way for him to enter the great game of the world. I may wish to change the rules of the game, as the revolutionary does, or to make an exception for myself, as the criminal does; but to deny them on principle means no mere "disobedience," but the refusal to enter the human community. The common dilemma—either the law is absolutely valid and therefore needs for its legitimacy an immortal, divine legislator, or the law is simply a command with nothing behind it but the state's monopoly of violence—is a delusion. All laws are " 'directives' rather than 'imperatives.' " They direct human intercourse as the rules direct the game. And the ultimate guarantee of their validity is contained in the old Roman maxim *Pacta sunt servanda.*

XII, TO PAGE 149, NOTE 72

There is some controversy on the purpose of de Gaulle's visit. The evidence of the events themselves seems to suggest that the price he had to pay for the army's support was public rehabilitation of his enemies—amnesty for General Salan, return of Bidault, return also of Colonel Lacheroy, sometimes called the "torturer in Algeria." Not much seems to be known about the negotiations. One is tempted to think that the recent rehabilitation of Pétain, again glorified as the "victor of Verdun," and, more importantly, de Gaulle's incredible, blatantly lying statement immediately after his return, blaming the Communist party for what the French now call *les événements,* were part of the bargain. God knows, the only reproach the government could have addressed to the Communist party and the trade unions was that they lacked the power to prevent *les événements.*

XIII, TO PAGE 153, NOTE 75

It would be interesting to know if, and to what an extent, the alarming rate of unsolved crimes is matched not only by the well-known spectacular rise in criminal offenses but also by a definite increase in police brutality. The recently published *Uniform Crime Report for the United States,* by J. Edgar Hoover (Federal Bureau of Investigation, United States Department of Justice, 1967), gives no indication how many crimes are actually solved—as distinguished from "cleared by arrest"—but does mention in the Summary that police solutions of serious crimes declined in 1967 by 8%. Only 21.7 (or 21.9)% of all crimes are "cleared by arrest," and of these only 75% could be turned over to the courts, where only about 60% of the indicted were found guilty! Hence, the odds in favor of the criminal are so high that the constant rise in criminal offenses seems only natural. Whatever the causes for the spectacular decline of police efficiency, the decline of police power is evident, and with it the likelihood of brutality increases. Students and other demonstrators are like sitting ducks for police who have become used to hardly ever catching a criminal.

A comparison of the situation with that of other countries is difficult because of the different statistical methods employed. Still, it appears that, though the rise of undetected crime seems to be a fairly general problem, it has nowhere reached such alarming proportions as in America. In Paris, for instance, the rate of solved crimes declined from 62% in 1967 to 56% in 1968, in Germany from 73.4% in 1954 to 52.2% in 1967, and in Sweden 41% of crimes were solved in 1967. (See "Deutsche Polizei," in *Der Spiegel*, April 7, 1967.)

XIV, TO PAGE 154, NOTE 76

Solzhenitsyn shows in concrete detail how attempts at a rational economic development were wrecked by Stalin's methods, and one hopes this book will put to rest the myth that terror and the enormous losses in human lives were the price that had to be paid for rapid industrialization of the country. Rapid progress was made after Stalin's death, and what is striking in Russia today is that the country is still backward in comparison not only with the West but also with most of the satellite countries. In Russia there seems not much illusion left on this point, if there ever was any. The younger generation, especially the veterans of the Second World War, knows very well that only a miracle saved Russia from defeat in 1941, and that this miracle was the brutal fact that the enemy turned out to be even worse than the native ruler. What then turned the scales was that police terror abated under the pressure of the national emergency; the people, left to themselves, could again gather together and generate enough power to defeat the foreign invader. When they returned from prisoner-of-war camps or from occupation duty they were promptly sent for long years to labor and concentration camps in order to break them of the habits of freedom. It is precisely this generation, which tasted freedom during the war and terror afterward, that is challenging the tyranny of the present regime.

XV, TO PAGE 163, NOTE 86

No one in his right senses can believe—as certain German student groups recently theorized—that only when the government has been forced "to practice violence openly" will the rebels be able "to fight against this shit society (*Scheissgesellschaft*) with adequate means and destroy it." (Quoted in *Der Spiegel*, February 10, 1969, p. 30.) This linguistically (though hardly intellectually) vulgarized new version of the old Communist nonsense of the thirties, that the victory of fascism was all to the good for those who were against it, is either sheer play-acting, the "revolutionary" variant of hypocrisy, or testifies to the political idiocy of "believers." Except that forty years ago it was Stalin's deliberate pro-Hitler policy and not just stupid theorizing that stood behind it.

To be sure, there is no reason for being particularly surprised that German students are more given to theorizing and less gifted in political action and judgment than their colleagues in other, politically more fortunate, countries; nor that "the isolation of intelligent and vital minds . . . in Germany" is more pronounced, the polarization more desperate, than elsewhere, and their impact upon the political climate of their own country, except for backlash phenomena, almost nil. I also would agree with Spender (see "The Berlin Youth Model," in *op. cit.*) about the role played in this situation by the still-recent past, so that the students "are resented, not just on account of their violence, but because they are reminders . . . they also have the look of ghosts risen from hastily covered graves." And yet, when all this has been said and duly taken into account, there remains the strange and disquieting fact that none of the new leftist groups in Germany, whose vociferous opposition to nationalist or imperialist policies of other countries has been notoriously extremist, has concerned itself seriously with the recognition of the Oder-Neisse Line, which, after all, is the crucial issue of German foreign policy and the touchstone of German nationalism since the defeat of the Hitler regime.

XVI, TO PAGE 170, NOTE 99

Daniel Bell is cautiously hopeful because he is aware that scientific and technical work depend on "theoretical knowledge [that] is sought, tested, and codified in a disinterested way" (*op. cit*). Perhaps this optimism can be justified so long as the scientists and technologists remain uninterested in power and are concerned with no more than social prestige, that is, so long as they neither rule nor govern. Noam Chomsky's pessimism, "neither history nor psychology nor sociology gives us any particular reason to look forward with hope to the rule of the new mandarins," may be excessive; there are as yet no historical precedents, and the scientists and intellectuals who, with such deplorable regularity, have been found willing to serve every government that happened to be in power, have been no "meritocrats" but, rather, social climbers. But Chomsky is entirely right in raising the question: "Quite generally, what grounds are there for supposing that those whose claim to power is based on knowledge and technique will be more benign in their exercise of power than those whose claim is based on wealth or aristocratic origin?" (*Op. cit.*, p. 27.) And there is every reason to raise the complementary question: What grounds are there for supposing that the resentment against a meritocracy, whose rule is exclusively based on "natural" gifts, that is, on brain power, will be no more dangerous, no more violent than the resentment of earlier oppressed groups who at least had the consolation that their condition was caused by no "fault" of their own? Is it not plausible to assume that this resentment will harbor all the murderous traits of a racial antagonism, as distinguished from mere class conflicts, inasmuch as it too will concern natural data which cannot be changed, hence a condition from which one could liberate oneself only by extermination of those who happen to have a higher I.Q.? And since in such a constellation the numerical power of the disadvantaged will be overwhelming and social mobility almost nil, is it not likely that the danger of demagogues, of popular leaders, will be so great that the meritocracy will be forced into tyrannies and despotism?

XVII, TO PAGE 174, NOTE 106

Stewart Alsop, in a perceptive column, "The Wallace Man," in *Newsweek*, October 21, 1968, makes the point: "It may be illiberal of the Wallace man not to want to send his children to bad schools in the name of integration, but it is not at all unnatural. And it is not unnatural either for him to worry about the 'molestation' of his wife, or about losing his equity in his house, which is all he has!" He also quotes the most effective statement of George Wallace's demagoguery: "There are 535 members of Congress and a lot of these liberals have children, too. You know how many send their kids to the public schools in Washington? Six."

Another prime example of ill-designed integration policies was recently published by Neil Maxwell in *The Wall Street Journal* (August 8, 1968). The federal government promotes school integration in the South by cutting off federal funds in cases of flagrant noncompliance. In one such instance, $200,000 of annual aid was withheld. "Of the total, $175,000 went directly to Negro schools. . . . Whites promptly raised taxes to replace the other $25,000." In short, what is supposed to help Negro education actually has a "crushing impact" on their existing school system and no impact at all on white schools.

XVIII, TO PAGE 178, NOTE 110

In the murky climate of ideological talk and doubletalk of Western student debate, these issues seldom have a chance of being clarified; indeed, "this community, verbally so radical, has always sought and found an escape," in the words of Günter Grass. It is also true that this is especially noticeable and infuriating in German students and other members of the New Left. "They don't know anything, but they know it all," as a young historian in Prague, according to Grass, summed it up. Hans Magnus Enzensberger gives voice to the general German attitude; the Czechs suffer from "an extremely limited horizon. Their political substance is meager." (See Günter Grass, *op. cit.*, pp. 138-142.) In contrast to this mixture of stupidity and impertinence, the atmosphere among the eastern rebels is refreshing, although one shudders to think of the exorbitant price that has been paid for it. Jan Kavan, a Czech student leader, writes: "I have often been told by my friends in western Europe that we are only fighting for bourgeois-democratic freedoms. But somehow I cannot seem to distinguish between capitalist freedoms and socialist freedoms. What I recognize are basic human freedoms." (*Ramparts,* September 1968.) It is safe to assume that he would have a similar difficulty with the distinction between "progressive and repressive violence." However, it would be wrong to conclude, as is so frequently done, that people in the western countries have no legitimate complaints precisely in the matter of freedom. To be sure, it is only natural "that the attitude of the Czech to the western students is largely coloured by envy" (quoted from a student paper by Spender, *op. cit.*, p. 72), but it is also true that they lack certain, less brutal and yet very decisive experiences in political frustration.

Thoughts on Politics
and Revolution
A Commentary

This essay is based on an interview with Miss Arendt by the German writer Adelbert Reif, which took place in the summer of 1970. It has been translated by Denver Lindley.

QUESTION: In your study *On Violence* at several points you take up the question of the revolutionary student movement in the Western countries. In the end, though, one thing remains unclear: Do you consider the student protest movement in general a historically positive process?

ARENDT: I don't know what you mean by "positive." I assume you mean, am I for it or against it. Well, I welcome some of the goals of the movement, especially in America, where I am better acquainted with them than elsewhere; toward others I take a neutral attitude, and some I consider dangerous nonsense—as, for example, politicizing and "refunctioning" (what the Germans call *umfunktionieren*) the universities, that is, perverting their function, and other things of that sort. But not the right of participation. Within certain limits I thoroughly approve of that. But I don't want to go into that question for the moment.

If I disregard all the national differences, which of course are very great, and only take into account that this is a global movement—something that has never existed before in this form—and if I consider what (apart from

201

goals, opinions, doctrines) really distinguishes this generation in all countries from earlier generations, then the first thing that strikes me is its determination to act, its joy in action, the assurance of being able to change things by one's own efforts. This, of course, is expressed very differently in different countries according to their various political situations and historical traditions, which in turn means according to their very different political talents. But I would like to take that up later.

Let us look briefly at the beginnings of this movement. It arose in the United States quite unexpectedly in the fifties, at the time of the so-called "silent generation," the apathetic, undemonstrative generation. The immediate cause was the civil-rights movement in the South, and the first to join it were students from Harvard, who then attracted students from other famous eastern universities. They went to the South, organized brilliantly, and for a time had a quite extraordinary success, so long, that is, as it was simply a question of changing the climate of opinion —which they definitely succeeded in doing in a short time— and doing away with certain laws and ordinances in the Southern states; in short, so long as it was a question of purely legal and political matters. Then they collided with the enormous social needs of the city ghettos in the North —and there they came to grief, there they could accomplish nothing.

It was only later, after they had actually accomplished what could be accomplished through purely political action, that the business with the universities began. It started in Berkeley with the Free Speech Movement and continued with the Anti-War Movement, and again the results have been quite extraordinary. From these beginnings and especially from these successes springs everything that has since spread around the world.

In America this new assurance that one can change things one doesn't like is conspicuous especially in small matters. A typical instance was a comparatively harmless confrontation some years ago. When students learned that the service employees of their university were not receiving standard wages, they struck—with success. Basically it was an act of solidarity with "their" university against the policy of the administration. Or, to take another instance, in 1970 university students demanded time off in order to be able to take part in the election campaign, and a number of the larger universities granted them this free time. This is a political activity *outside the university* which is made possible by the university in recognition of the fact that students are citizens as well. I consider both instances definitely positive. There are, however, other things I consider far less positive, and we will get to them later.

The basic question is: What really did happen? As I see it, for the first time in a very long while a spontaneous political movement arose which not only did not simply carry on propaganda, but acted, *and, moreover, acted almost exclusively from moral motives.* Together with this moral factor, quite rare in what is usually considered a mere power or interest play, another experience new for our time entered the game of politics: It turned out that acting is fun. This generation discovered what the eighteenth century had called "public happiness," which means that when man takes part in public life he opens up for himself a dimension of human experience that otherwise remains closed to him and that in some way constitutes a part of complete "happiness."

In all these matters I would rate the student movement as very positive. Its further development is another question. How long the so-called "positive" factors will hold good, whether they are not already in process of being dissolved, eaten away by fanaticism, ideologies, and a destructiveness that often borders on the criminal, on one side, by boredom, on the other, no one knows. The good things in history are usually of very short duration, but afterward have a decisive influence on what happens over long periods of time. Just consider how short the true classical period in Greece was, and that we are in effect still nourished by it today.

Q: Ernst Bloch recently pointed out in a lecture that the student protest movement is not confined to its known objectives but contains principles derived from the old natural law: "Men who do not truckle, who do not flatter the whims of their masters." Now Bloch says that the students have brought back into consciousness "this other subversive element of revolution," which must be distinguished from simple protest at a bad economic situation, and in so doing have made an important contribution "to the history of revolutions and very likely to the structure of the coming revolutions." What is your opinion?

A: What Ernst Bloch calls "natural law" is what I was referring to when I spoke of the conspicuous moral coloration of the movement. However, I would add—and on this point I am not in agreement with Bloch—that something similar was the case with all revolutionaries. If you look at the history of revolutions, you will see that it was never the oppressed and degraded themselves who led the way, but those who were not oppressed and not degraded but could not bear it that others were. Only, they were embarrassed to admit their moral motives—and this shame is very old. I don't want to go into the history of it here, though it has a very interesting aspect. But the moral factor has always been present, although it finds clearer expres-

204

sion today because people are not ashamed to own up to it.

As for the business of "not truckling," naturally it plays an especially important role in those countries, like Japan and Germany, where obsequiousness had grown to such formidable proportions, while in America, where I cannot recollect a single student ever having truckled, it is really rather meaningless. I have already mentioned that this international movement naturally takes on different national colorations, and that these colorations, simply because they are colorings, are sometimes the most striking thing; it is easy, especially for an outsider, to mistake what is most conspicuous for what is most important.

On the question of "the coming revolution" in which Ernst Bloch believes and about which I do not know whether it will come at all or what structure it might have if it did, I would like to say this: There are, it is true, a whole series of phenomena of which one can say at once that in the light of our experience (which after all is not very old, but dates only from the French and American Revolutions; before that there were rebellions and *coups d'état* but no revolutions) they belong to the prerequisites of revolution—such as the threatened breakdown of the machinery of government, its being undermined, the loss of confidence in the government on the part of the people, the failure of public services, and various others.

The loss of power and authority by all the great powers is clearly visible, even though it is accompanied by an immense accumulation of the means of violence in the hands of the governments, but the increase in weapons cannot compensate for the loss of power. Nevertheless, this situation need not lead to revolution. For one thing, it can end in counterrevolution, the establishment of dictatorships, and, for another, it can end in total anticlimax: it need not lead to anything. No one alive today knows anything about a coming revolution: "the principle of hope" (Ernst Bloch) certainly gives no sort of guarantee.

At the moment, one prerequisite for a coming revolution is lacking: a group of real revolutionaries. Just what the students on the left would most like to be—revolutionaries—that is just what they are not. Nor are they organized as revolutionaries: they have no inkling of what power means, and if power were lying in the street and they knew it was lying there, they are certainly the last to be ready to stoop down and pick it up. That is precisely what revolutionaries do. Revolutionaries do not make revolutions! The revolutionaries are those who know when power is lying in the street and when they can pick it up. Armed uprising by itself has never yet led to a revolution.

Nevertheless, what could pave the way for a revolution, in the sense of preparing the revolutionaries, is a real analysis of the existing situation such as used to be made in earlier times. To be sure, even then these analyses were mostly very inadequate, but the fact remains that they were made. In this respect I see absolutely no one, near or far, in a position to do this. The theoretical sterility and analytical dullness of this movement are just as striking and depressing as its joy in action is welcome. In Germany the movement is also rather helpless in practical matters; it can cause some rioting, but aside from the shouting of slogans it can organize nothing. In America, where on certain occasions it has brought out hundreds of thousands to demonstrate in Washington, the movement is in this respect, in its ability to act, most impressive! But the mental sterility is the same in both countries—only, in Germany, where people are so fond of loose, theoretical talk, they go about peddling obsolete conceptions and categories mainly derived from the nineteenth century, or beat you about the head with them, as the case may be. None of this bears any relationship to modern conditions. And none of this has anything to do with reflection.

Things are different, to be sure, in South America and in Eastern Europe, principally because there has been vastly more concrete practical experience there. But to examine this in detail would take us too far afield.

I would like to talk about one other point that occurred to me in connection with Ernst Bloch and "the principle of hope." The most suspicious thing about this movement in Western Europe and America is a curious despair involved in it, as though its adherents already knew they would be smashed. And as though they said to themselves: At least we want to have provoked our defeat; we do not want, in addition to everything else, to be as innocent as lambs. There is an element of running amok on the part of these bomb-throwing children. I have read that French students in Nanterre during the last disturbances—not the ones in 1968, but the recent ones—wrote on the walls: "Ne gâchez pas votre pourriture" ("Don't spoil your rottenness"). Right on, right on. This conviction that everything deserves to be destroyed, that everybody deserves to go to hell—this sort of desperation can be detected everywhere, though it is less pronounced in America, where "the principle of hope" is yet unknown, perhaps because people don't yet need it so desperately.

Q: Do you see the student protest movement in the United States as essentially frustrated?

A: By no means. The successes it has so far achieved are too great. Its success with the Negro question is spectacular, and its success in the matter of the war is perhaps even greater. It was primarily the students who succeeded in dividing the country, and ended with a majority, or at all events a very strong, highly qualified minority, against the war. It could, however, very quickly come to ruin if it actually succeeded in destroying the universities—something I consider possible. In America, perhaps this danger is less than elsewhere because American students are still more oriented toward political questions and less toward internal university problems, with the result that a part of the populace feels solidarity with them on essential matters. But in America, too, it is still conceivable that the universities will be destroyed, for the whole disturbance coincides with a crisis in the sciences, in belief in science, and in belief in progress, that is, with an internal, not simply a political, crisis of the universities.

If the students should succeed in destroying the universities, then they will have destroyed their own base of operations—and this would be true in all the countries affected, in America as well as in Europe. Nor will they be able to find another base, simply because they cannot come together anywhere else. It follows that the destruction of the universities would spell the end of the whole movement.

But it would not be the end either of the educational system or of research. Both can be organized quite differently; other forms and institutions for professional training and research are perfectly conceivable. But then there will be no more college students. Let us ask what in fact is student freedom. The universities make it possible for young people over a number of years *to stand outside all social groups and obligations,* to be truly free. If the students destroy the universities, then nothing of the sort will any longer exist; consequently there will be no rebellion against society either. In some countries and at some times, they have been well on their way to sawing off the branch they are sitting on. That in turn is connected with running

208

amok. In this way the student protest movement could in fact not only fail to gain its demands but could also be destroyed.

Q: Would that hold good, too, for the student protest movement in Europe?

A: Yes, it would apply to most student movements. Once more, not so much to those in South America and in the Eastern European countries, where the protest movement is not directly dependent on the universities and where a large part of the population is behind it.

Q: In your study *On Violence*, there is this sentence: "The third world is not a reality but an ideology." That sounds like blasphemy. For, of course, the third world is a reality; what's more, a reality that was brought into being first by the Western colonial powers and later with the co-operation of the United States. And so it is not at all surprising that this reality produced by capitalism should result, under the influence of the world-wide and general indignation of youth, in a new ideology. However, the significant thing, I believe, is not this ideology of the New Left, but simply the existence of the third world, the reality of the third world, which first made this ideology possible.

Do you really intend by your astonishing sentence to question the reality of the third world as such? Possibly there's a misunderstanding here that you could clear up.

A: Not a bit of it. I am truly of the opinion that the third world is exactly what I said, an ideology or an illusion.

Africa, Asia, South America—those are realities. If you now compare these regions with Europe and America,

then you can say of them—but only from this perspective—
that they are underdeveloped, and you assert thereby that
this is a crucial common denominator between these countries. However, you overlook the innumerable things they
do *not* have in common, and the fact that what they do
have in common is only a contrast that exists with another
world; which means that the idea of underdevelopment as
the important factor is a European-American prejudice.
The whole thing is simply a question of perspective; there
is a logical fallacy here. Try telling a Chinese sometime
that he belongs to exactly the same world as an African
Bantu tribesman and, believe me, you'll get the surprise of
your life. The only ones who have an obviously political
interest in saying that there is a third world are, of course,
those who stand on the lowest step—that is, the Negroes in
Africa. In their case it's easy to understand; all the rest is
empty talk.

The New Left has borrowed the catchword of the third
world from the arsenal of the Old Left. It has been taken
in by the distinction made by the imperialists between
colonial countries and colonizing powers. For the imperialists, Egypt was, naturally, like India: they both fell under
the heading of "subject races." This imperialist leveling
out of all differences is copied by the New Left, only with
labels reversed. It is always the same old story: being taken
in by every catchword, the inability to think or else the unwillingness to see phenomena as they really are, without
applying categories to them in the belief that they can
thereby be classified. It is just this that constitutes theoretical helplessness.

The new slogan—Natives of all colonies, or of all former
colonies or of all underdeveloped countries, unite!—is even
crazier than the old one from which it was copied: Work-

ers of the world, unite!—which, after all, has been thoroughly discredited. I am certainly not of the opinion that one can learn very much from history—for history constantly confronts us with what is new—but there are a couple of small things that it should be possible to learn. What fills me with such misgivings is that I do not see anywhere people of this generation recognizing realities as such, and taking the trouble to think about them.

Q: Marxist philosophers and historians, and not just those in the strict sense of the word, today take the view that in this stage of the historical development of mankind there are only two possible alternatives for the future: capitalism or socialism. In your view, does another alternative exist?

A: I see no such alternatives in history; nor do I know what is in store there. Let's not talk about such grand matters as "the historical development of mankind"—in all likelihood it will take a turn that corresponds neither to the one nor to the other, and let us hope it will come as a surprise to us.

But let's look at your alternatives historically for a moment: it began, after all, with capitalism, an economic system that no one had planned and no one had foreseen. This system, as is generally known, owed its start to a monstrous process of expropriation such as has never occurred before in history in this form—that is, without military conquest. Expropriation, the initial accumulation of capital—that was the law according to which capitalism arose and according to which it has advanced step by step. Now just what people imagine by socialism I do not know. But if you look at what has actually happened in Russia, then you can see that there the process of expropriation has been carried further; and you can observe that something very similar is going on in the modern capitalistic countries, where it is as though the old expropriation process is again let loose. Overtaxation, a *de facto* devaluation of currency, inflation coupled with a recession—what else are these but relatively mild forms of expropriation?

Only in the Western countries are there political and legal obstacles that constantly keep this process of expropriation from reaching the point where life would be completely unbearable. In Russia there is, of course, not socialism, but state socialism, which is the same thing as state capitalism would be—that is, total expropriation. Total expropriation occurs when all political and legal safeguards of private ownership have disappeared. In Russia, for instance, certain groups enjoy a very high standard of living. The trouble is only that whatever these people may have at their disposition—cars, country houses, expensive furniture, chauffeur-driven limousines, et cetera—they do not own; it can be taken away from them by the government any day. No man there is so rich that he cannot be made a beggar overnight—without even the right to employment—in case of any conflict with the ruling powers. (One glance into recent Soviet literature, where people have started to tell the truth, will testify to the atrocious consequences more tellingly than all economic and political theories.)

All our experiences—as distinguished from theories and ideologies—tell us that the process of expropriation, which started with the rise of capitalism, does not stop with the expropriation of the means of production; only legal and political institutions that are independent of the economic forces and their automatism can control and check the inherently monstrous potentialities of this process. Such political controls seem to function best in the so-called "welfare states" whether they call themselves "socialist" or "capitalist." What protects freedom is the division between governmental and economic power, or, to put it into Marxian language, the fact that the state and its constitution are not superstructures.

What protects us in the so-called "capitalist" countries of the West is not capitalism, but a legal system that prevents the daydreams of big-business management of trespassing into the private sphere of its employees from coming true. But this dream does come true wherever the government itself becomes the employer. It is no secret that the clearance system for American government employees does not respect private life; the recent appetite of certain governmental agencies to bug private homes could also be seen as an attempt on the part of the government to treat all citizens as prospective government employees. And what else is bugging but a form of expropriation? The government agency establishes itself as a kind of co-owner of the apartments and houses of citizens. In Russia no fancy gadgets in the walls are necessary; there, a spy sits in every citizen's apartment anyhow.

If I were to judge these developments from a Marxian viewpoint, I would say: Perhaps expropriation is indeed in the very nature of modern production, and socialism is, as Marx believed, nothing but the inevitable result of industrial society as it was started by capitalism. Then the question is what can we do to get and keep this process under control so that it does not degenerate, under one name or another, into the monstrosities in which it has fallen in the East. In certain so-called "communist" countries—in Yugoslavia, for instance, but even in East Germany—there are attempts to decontrol and decentralize the economy, and very substantial concessions are being made in order to prevent the most horrifying consequences of the expropriation process, which, fortunately enough, also has turned out to be very unsatisfactory for production once a certain point of centralization and enslavement of the workers has been reached.

Fundamentally it is a question of how much property and how many rights we can allow a person to possess even under the very inhuman conditions of much of modern economy. But nobody can tell me that there is such a thing as workers "owning their factories." Collective ownership is, if you reflect for a second, a contradiction in terms. Property is what belongs to me; ownership relates to what is my own by definition. Other people's means of production should not, of course, belong to me; they might perhaps be controlled by a third authority, which means they belong to no one. The worst possible owner would be the government, unless its powers in this economic sphere are strictly controlled and checked by a truly independent judiciary. Our problem today is not how to expropriate the expropriators, but, rather, how to arrange matters so that the masses, dispossessed by industrial society in capitalist and socialist systems, can regain property. For this reason alone, the alternative between capitalism and socialism is false—not only because neither exists anywhere in its pure state anyhow, but because we have here twins, each wearing a different hat.

The same state of affairs can be looked at from a different perspective—from that of the oppressed themselves—which does not make the result any better. In that case one must say that capitalism has destroyed the estates, the corporations, the guilds, the whole structure of feudal society. It has done away with all the collective groups which were a protection for the individual and for his property, which guaranteed him a certain security, though not, of course, complete safety. In their place it has put the "classes," essentially just two: the exploiters and the exploited. Now the working class, simply because it was a class and a collective, still provided the individual with a certain protection, and later, when it learned to organize, it fought for and secured considerable rights for itself. The chief distinction today is not between socialist and capitalist countries but between countries that respect these rights, as, for instance, Sweden on one side, the United States on the other, and those that do not, as, for instance, Franco's Spain on one side, Soviet Russia on the other.

What then has socialism or communism, taken in its pure form, done? It has destroyed this class, too, its institutions, the unions and the labor parties, and its rights—collective bargaining, strikes, unemployment insurance, social security. In their stead, these regimes offered the illusion that the factories were the property of the working class, which as a class had just been abolished, and the atrocious lie that unemployment no longer existed, a lie based on nothing but the very real nonexistence of unemployment insurance. In essence, socialism has simply continued, and driven to its extreme, what capitalism began. Why should it be the remedy?

Q: Marxist intellectuals often emphasize that socialism, in spite of alienation, is always capable of regeneration through its own strength. As an ideal example of this regeneration there is the Czechoslovakian model of democratic socialism.

In view of the increase in military weapons by the Soviet Union and Soviet hegemony in other areas as well, how do you judge the chances of a new initiative for democratic socialism in the East, oriented in the spirit of the Czechoslovakian or Yugoslavian models?

A: What you just said in your first sentence really shocked me. To call Stalin's rule an "alienation" seems to me a euphemism used to sweep under the rug not only facts, but the most hair-raising crimes as well. I say this to you simply to call your attention to how very much this jargon has already twisted the facts: To call something "alienation"—that is no less than a crime.

Now so far as economic systems and "models" are concerned, in time something will emerge from all the experimentation here and there if the great powers leave the small countries in peace. What that will be we cannot of course tell in a field so dependent on practice as economics. However, there will be experimentation first of all with the problem of ownership. On the basis of the very scanty information at my disposal, I would say that this is already happening in East Germany and in Yugoslavia with interesting results.

In East Germany, a kind of co-operative system, which does not derive at all from socialism and which has proved its worth in Denmark and in Israel, has been built into the "socialistic" economic system—thereby making it work. In Yugoslavia we have the "system of self-management" in the factories, a new version of the old "workers' councils," which, incidentally, also never became part of orthodox socialist or communist doctrine—despite Lenin's "all power to the *soviets.*" (The councils, the only true outgrowth of the revolutions themselves as distinguished from revolutionary parties and ideologies, have been mercilessly destroyed precisely by the Communist party and by Lenin himself.)

None of these experiments redefines legitimate property in a satisfactory way, but they may be steps in this direction—the East German co-operatives by combining private ownership with the need for joint property in the means of production and distribution, the worker's councils by providing job security instead of the security of private property. In both instances individual workers are no longer atomized but belong to a new collective, the co-operative or the factory's council, as a kind of compensation for membership in a class.

You ask also about the experiments and reforms. These have nothing to do with economic systems—except that the economic system should not be used to deprive people of their freedom. This is done when a dissenter or opponent becomes "unemployable" or when consumer goods are so scarce and life so uncomfortable that it is easy for the government to "buy" whole sections of the population. What people in the East do care about are freedom, civil rights, legal guarantees. For these are the conditions for being free to say, to write, and to print whatever one likes. The Soviet Union marched into Czechoslovakia not because of the new "economic model" but because of the *political* reforms connected with it. It did not march into East Germany, although today people there, as in other satellite countries, live better than in the Soviet Union and perhaps soon will live just as well and eventually even better than those in West Germany. And then the difference will be "only" that in one country people can say and, within limits, also do what they like and in the other they cannot. Believe me, *that* makes an enormous difference to everyone.

The Soviet Union has an interest in striking home wherever these economic experiments are joined to a struggle for freedom. Without doubt this was the case in Czechoslovakia. It is not the case in East Germany; therefore the German Democratic Republic is left in peace. Under Ulbricht's rule, the German Democratic Republic has become constantly more tyrannical ideologically the greater its economic concessions.

The Soviet Union must also strike home whenever it

fears that one of the satellite countries is breaking away from the Warsaw Pact. Whether this fear, certainly present, was justified in the case of Czechoslovakia I do not know, but I consider it possible. On the other hand, I do not believe that the Soviet Union will intervene militarily in Yugoslavia. It would encounter there a very considerable military opposition, and it cannot today afford this kind of confrontation. It is not that firmly seated in the saddle, being a great power.

Q: Do you give socialism as the dominant conception at present for the future of human society any chance of realization?

A: This naturally brings up the question again of what socialism really is. Even Marx hardly knew what he should concretely picture by that.

Q: If I may interrupt: What is meant is socialism, as I said before, oriented in the spirit of the Czechoslovakian or Yugoslavian model.

A: You mean, then, what today is called "socialistic humanism." This new slogan means no more than the attempt to undo the inhumanity brought about by socialism without reintroducing a so-called "capitalist" system, although the clear tendency in Yugoslavia toward an open market economy could very easily, and almost certainly will, be so interpreted, not only by the Soviet Union, but by all true believers.

Generally speaking, I would say that I grant a chance to all the small countries that want to experiment, whether they call themselves socialist or not, but I am very skeptical about the great powers. These mass societies can no longer be controlled, let alone governed. The Czechoslovakian and Yugoslavian models, if you take these two as examples, naturally have a chance. I would also include perhaps Rumania, perhaps Hungary, where the revolution did not by any means end catastrophically, as it might have ended under Stalin—simply with the deportation of 50 per cent of the population. In all these countries something is going on, and it will be very hard to reverse their reform efforts, their attempts to escape from the worst consequences of dictatorship and to solve their economic problems independently and sensibly.

There is another factor we should take into account. The Soviet Union and, in various degrees, its satellite states are not nation-states, but are composed of nationalities. In each of them, the dictatorship is more or less in the hands of the dominant nationality, and the opposition against it always risks turning into a national liberation movement. This is especially true in the Soviet Union, where the Russian dictators always live in the fear of a collapse of the Russian empire—and not just a change of government.

This concern has nothing to do with socialism; it is, and always has been, an issue of sheer power politics. I don't think that the Soviet Union would have proceeded as it did in Czechoslovakia if it had not been worried about its own inner opposition, not only the opposition of the intellectuals, but the latent opposition of its own nationalities. One should not forget that during the Prague Spring the government granted considerable concessions to the Slovaks which only recently, certainly under Russian influence, were canceled. All attempts at decentralization are feared by Moscow. A new model—this means, to the Russians, not only a more humane handling of the economic or intellectual questions but also the threat of the decomposition of the Russian empire.

Q: I think the Soviet leaders' fear, specifically of the opposition of the intellectuals, plays a special role. After all, it is an opposition that today is making itself felt in a wider field. There is even a civil-rights movement on the part of young intellectuals which operates with all available legal and, needless to say, also illegal means, such as underground newspapers, et cetera.

A: Yes, I am aware of that. And the leaders of the Soviet Union are naturally very much afraid of it. They are very much afraid that if the success of this movement extends to the people, as distinguished from the intellectuals, it could mean that the Ukrainians would once more want to have a state of their own, likewise the Tartars, who in any case were so abominably treated, and so on. Therefore the rulers of the Soviet Union are on an even shakier footing than the rulers in the satellite countries. But you see, too, that Tito in Yugoslavia is afraid of the problem of nationalities and not at all of so-called "capitalism."

Q: How do you account for the fact that the reform movement in the East—I am thinking not only of the much-cited Czechoslovakian model, but also of various publications by Soviet intellectuals advocating democratization of the Soviet Union, and similar protests—never put forward any form of capitalism, however modified, as an alternative to the system they are criticizing.

A: Well, I could say to you that these people are obviously of my opinion, that just as socialism is no remedy for capitalism, capitalism cannot be a remedy or an alternative for socialism. But I will not harp on that. The contest is never simply over an economic system. The economic system is involved only so far as a dictatorship hinders the economy from developing as productively as it would without dictatorial constraint. For the rest, it has to do with the political question: It has to do with what kind of state one wants to have, what kind of constitution, what kind of legislation, what sort of safeguards for the freedom of the spoken and printed word; that is, it has to do with what our innocent children in the West call "bourgeois freedom."

There is no such thing; freedom is freedom whether guaranteed by the laws of a "bourgeois" government or a "communist" state. From the fact that communist governments today do not respect civil rights and do not guarantee freedom of speech and association it does not follow that such rights and freedoms are "bourgeois." "Bourgeois freedom" is frequently and quite wrongly equated with the freedom to make more money than one actually needs. For this is the only "freedom" which the East, where in fact one can become extremely rich, respects, too. The contrast between rich and poor—if we are to talk a sensible language for once and not jargon—in respect to income is greater in the East than in most other countries, greater even than in the United States if you disregard a few thousand multimillionaires.

But that is not the point either. I repeat: The point is simply and singly whether I can say and print what I wish, or whether I cannot; whether my neighbors spy on me or don't. Freedom always implies freedom of dissent. No ruler before Stalin and Hitler contested the freedom to say yes—Hitler excluding Jews and gypsies from the right to consent and Stalin having been the only dictator who chopped off the heads of his most enthusiastic supporters, perhaps because he figured that whoever says yes can also say no. No tyrant before them went that far—and that did not pay off either.

None of these systems, not even that of the Soviet Union, is still truly totalitarian—though I have to admit that I am not in a position to judge China. At present only the people who dissent and are in the opposition are excluded, but this does not signify by any means that there is any freedom there. And it is precisely in political freedom and assured basic rights that the opposition forces are interested—and rightly so.

Q: How do you stand on Thomas Mann's statement "Anti-bolshevism is the basic foolishness of our time"?

A: There are so many absurdities in our time that it is hard to assign first place. But, to speak seriously, antibolshevism as a theory, as an ism, is the invention of the ex-communists. By that I do not mean just any former bolsheviks or communists, but, rather, those who *"believed"* and then one day were personally disillusioned by Mr. Stalin; that is, people who were not really revolutionaries or politically engaged but who, as they themselves said, had lost a god and then went in search of a new god and also the opposite, a new devil. They simply reversed the pattern.

But to say that the mentality of these people changed, that instead of searching for beliefs they saw realities, took them into account, and attempted to change things is erroneous. Whether antibolshevists announce that the East is the devil, or bolshevists maintain that America is the devil, as far as their habits of thought go it amounts to the same thing. The mentality is still the same. It sees only black and white. In reality there is no such thing. If one does not know the whole spectrum of political colors of an epoch, cannot distinguish between the basic conditions of the different countries, the various stages of development, traditions, kinds and grades in production, technology, mentality, and so on, then one simply does not know how to move and take one's bearings in this field. One can do nothing but smash the world to bits in order finally to have before one's eyes one thing: plain black.

Q: At the end of *On Violence,* you write that we know "or should know that every decrease of power is an open invitation to violence—if only because those who hold power and feel it slipping from their hands . . . have always found it difficult to resist the temptation to substitute violence for it." What does this weighty sentence mean in respect to the present political situation in the United States?

A: I spoke earlier about the loss of power on the part of the great powers. If we consider this concretely, what does it mean? In all republics with representative governments, power resides in the people. That means that the people empower certain individuals to represent them, to act in their name. When we talk about loss of power, that signifies that the people have withdrawn their consent from what their representatives, the empowered elected officials, do.

Those who have been empowered naturally feel powerful; even when the people withdraw the basis of that power, the feeling of power remains. That is the situation in America—not only there, to be sure. This state of affairs, incidentally, has nothing to do with the fact that the people are divided, but, rather, is to be explained by loss of confidence in the so-called "system." In order to maintain the system, the empowered ones begin to act as rulers and resort to force. They substitute force for the assent of the people; that is the turning point.

How does this stand in America at present? The matter can be illustrated by various examples, but I would like to elucidate it chiefly by the war in Vietnam, which not only actually divides the people in the United States but, even more important, has caused a loss of confidence and thereby a loss of power. To be specific, it has produced the "credibility gap," which means that those in power are no longer believed—quite apart from whether one agrees with them or not. I know that in Europe politicians never have been believed, that, indeed, people are of the opinion that politicians must and should lie as part of their trade. But that was not the case in America.

Naturally, there have always been state secrets which on specific grounds of practical politics needed to be strictly guarded. Often the truth was not told; but neither were direct lies. Now, as you know, the Gulf of Tonkin Resolution, which gave the President a free hand in an undeclared war, was forced through Congress on the basis of a provably inaccurate presentation of the circumstances. This affair cost Johnson the presidency; also, the bitterness of the opposition in the Senate can hardly be explained without it. Since that time, among widening circles, the Vietnam war has been considered illegal—not only peculiarly inhuman, not only immoral, but *illegal*. In America that has a different weight than in Europe.

Q: And yet among American labor there is very strong agitation *for* the engagement of the United States in Vietnam. How is that to be explained in this connection?

A: The first impetus of opposition to the war came from the universities, especially from the student body, that is, from the same groups that were engaged in the civil-rights movement. This opposition was directed from the beginning against the so-called "system," whose most loyal supporters today are unquestionably to be found among the workers, that is, in the lower-income groups. (On Wall Street the so-called "capitalists" demonstrated against the government and the construction workers for it.) In this, the decisive part was played not so much by the question of the war as by the color problem.

It has turned out that in the eastern and northern parts of the country integration of the Negroes into the higher-income groups encounters no very serious or insuperable difficulties. Today everywhere it is really a *fait accompli*. Dwellings with relatively high rentals can be integrated if the black tenants belong to the same upper level as the white or yellow (especially the Chinese, who are everywhere especially favored as neighbors). Since the number of successful black businessmen is very small, this really applies to the academic and liberal professions—doctors, lawyers, professors, actors, writers, and so on.

The same integration in the middle and lower levels of the middle class, and especially among the workers who in respect to income belong to the upper level of the lower middle class, leads to catastrophe, and this indeed not only because the lower middle class happens to be particularly "reactionary," but because these classes believe, not without reason, that all these reforms relating to the Negro problem are being carried out at their expense. This can best be illustrated by the example of the schools. Public schools in America, including high schools, are free. The better these schools are, the greater are the chances for children without means to get into the colleges and universities, that is, to improve their social position. In the big cities this public-school system, under the weight of a very numerous, almost exclusively black *Lumpenproletariat*, has with very few exceptions broken down; these institutions, in which children are kept for twelve years without even learning to read and write, can hardly be described as schools. Now if a section of the city becomes black as a result of the policy of integration, then the streets run to seed, the schools are neglected, the children run wild—in short, the neighborhood very quickly becomes a slum. The principal sufferers, aside from the blacks themselves, are the Italians, the Irish, the Poles, and other ethnic groups who are not poor but are not rich enough either to be able simply to move away or to send their children to the very expensive private schools.

This, however, is perfectly possible for the upper classes, though often at the cost of considerable sacrifice. People are perfectly right in saying that soon in New York only the very poor and the very rich will be able to live. Almost all the white residents who can do so send their children either to private schools, which are often very good, or to the principally Catholic denominational schools. Negroes belonging to the upper levels can also do this. The working class cannot, nor can the lower middle class. What makes these people especially bitter is that the middle-class liberals have put through laws whose consequences they do not feel. They demand integration of the public schools, elimination of neighborhood schools (black children, who in large measure are simply left to neglect, are transported in buses out of the slums into schools in predominantly white neighborhoods), forced integration of neighborhoods—and send their own children to private schools and move to the suburbs, something that only those at a certain income level can afford.

To this another factor is added, which is present in other countries as well. Marx may have said that the proletarian has no country; it is well known that the proletarians have never shared this point of view. The lower social classes are especially susceptible to nationalism, chauvinism, and imperialistic policies. One serious split in the civil-rights movement into "black" and "white" came as a result of the war question: the white students coming from good middle-class homes at once joined the opposition, in contrast to the Negroes, whose leaders were very slow in making up their minds to demonstrate against the war in Vietnam This was true even of Martin Luther King. The fact that the army gives the lower social classes certain opportunities for education and vocational training naturally also plays a role here.

Q: You reproach the New Left in West Germany with, among other things, having never "concerned itself seriously with the recognition of the Oder-Neisse Line, which, after all, is one of the crucial issues of German foreign policy and has been the touchstone of German nationalism ever since the defeat of the Hitler regime." I doubt that your thesis can be maintained in this uncompromising form, for the German New Left is also urging the recognition, not only of the Oder-Neisse Line by Bonn, but of the German Democratic Republic as well. However, the New Left is isolated from the general population, and it is not within its power to give practical political reality to such theoretical demands. But even if the numerically extremely weak New Left were to intervene "seriously" for the recognition of the Oder-Neisse Line would German nationalism thereby suffer a decisive defeat?

A: As far as practical political consequences are concerned, a change of policies in Persia was certainly even less likely. The trouble with the New Left is that it obviously cares about nothing less than eventual consequences of its demonstrations. In contrast to the Shah of Persia, the Oder-Neisse Line is a matter of direct responsibility for every German citizen; to demonstrate for its recognition and to go on record on this issue make sense regardless of practical political consequences. It proves nothing whatsoever if the New Left comes out "also" for the recognition of the new boundary with Poland—as many good liberal Germans have done. The point is that this issue has never been at the center of their propaganda, which means simply that they dodge all matters that are real and involve direct responsibility. This is true of their theories as well as of their practices.

There are two possible explanations for this shirking of an eminently practical issue. I have so far mentioned only German nationalism, of which, all rhetoric to the contrary notwithstanding, one might also suspect the New Left. The second possibility would be that this movement in its German version has indulged in so much high-flown theoretical nonsense that it cannot see what is in front of its nose. This seems to have been the case at the time of the Emergency Laws—the *Notstandsgesetze*. You remember how late the student movement was in becoming aware that something of considerable importance was happening in Parliament, certainly of greater importance for Germany than the visit of oriental potentates.

When the American students demonstrate against the war in Vietnam, they are demonstrating against a policy of immediate interest to their country and to themselves. When the German students do the same, it is pretty much as with the Shah of Persia; there is not the slightest possibility of their being personally held to account. Passionate interest in international affairs in which no risk and no responsibility are involved has often been a cloak to hide down-to-earth national interests; in politics, idealism is frequently no more than an excuse for not recognizing unpleasant realities. Idealism can be a form of evading reality altogether, and this, I think, is much more likely the case here. The New Left simply overlooked the issue, and that means it overlooked the single moral question that, in postwar Germany, was still really open and subject to debate. And it also overlooked one of the few decisive international political issues in which Germany would have been able to play a significant role after the end of World

War II. The failure of the German government, especially under Adenauer, to recognize the Oder-Neisse Line in time has contributed a great deal to the consolidation of the Soviet satellite system. It ought to be perfectly clear to everyone that fear of Germany on the part of the satellite nations has decisively slowed down, and in part rendered impossible, all reform movements in Eastern Europe. The fact that not even the Left, New or Old, dared to touch this most sensitive point of postwar Germany could only strengthen considerably this fear.

Q: To come back once more to your study *On Violence:* in it (that is, in its German version) you write: "So long as national independence, namely, freedom from foreign rule, and the sovereignty of the state, namely, the claim to unchecked and unlimited power in foreign affairs, are identified—and no revolution has thus far been able to shake this state concept—not even a theoretical solution of the problem of war, on which depends not so much the future of mankind as the question of whether mankind will have a future, is so much as conceivable, and a guaranteed peace on earth is as utopian as the squaring of the circle." What other conception of the state do you have in mind?

A: What I have in mind is not so much a different state concept as the necessity of changing this one. What we call the "state" is not much older than the fifteenth and sixteenth centuries, and the same thing is true of the concept of sovereignty. Sovereignty means, among other things, that conflicts of an international character can ultimately be settled only by war; there is no other last resort. Today, however, war—quite apart from all pacifist considerations—among the great powers has become impossible owing to the monstrous development of the means of violence. And so the question arises: What is to take the place of this last resort?

War has, so to speak, become a luxury which only the small nations can still afford, and they only so long as they are not drawn into the spheres of influence of the great powers and do not possess nuclear weapons themselves. The great powers interfere in these wars in part because they are obliged to defend their clients and in part because this has become an important piece of the strategy of mutual deterrence on which the peace of the world today rests.

Between sovereign states there can be no last resort except war; if war no longer serves that purpose, that fact alone proves that we must have a new concept of the state. This new concept of the state, to be sure, will not result from the founding of a new international court that would function better than the one at The Hague, or a new League of Nations, since the same conflicts between sovereign or ostensibly sovereign governments can only be played out there all over again—on the level of discourse, to be sure, which is more important than is usually thought.

The mere rudiments I see for a new state concept can be found in the federal system, whose advantage it is that power moves neither from above nor from below, but is horizontally directed so that the federated units mutually check and control their powers. For the real difficulty in speculating on these matters is that the final resort should not be *super*national but *inter*national. A supernational authority would either be ineffective or be monopolized by the nation that happens to be the strongest, and so would lead to world government, which could easily become the most frightful tyranny conceivable, since from its global police force there would be no escape—until it finally fell apart.

Where do we find models that could help us in construing, at least theoretically, an *inter*national authority as the highest control agency? This sounds like a paradox, since what is highest cannot well be in between, but it is nevertheless the real question. When I said that none of the revolutions, each of which overthrew one form of government and replaced it with another, had been able to shake the state concept and its sovereignty, I had in mind something that I tried to elaborate a bit in my book *On Revolution*. Since the revolutions of the eighteenth century, every large upheaval has actually developed the rudiments of an entirely new form of government, which emerged independent of all preceding revolutionary theories, directly out of the course of the revolution itself, that is, out of the experiences of action and out of the resulting will of the actors to participate in the further development of public affairs.

This new form of government is the council system, which, as we know, has perished every time and everywhere, destroyed either directly by the bureaucracy of the nation-states or by the party machines. Whether this system is a pure utopia—in any case it would be a people's utopia, not the utopia of theoreticians and ideologies—I cannot say. It seems to me, however, the single alternative that has ever appeared in history, and has reappeared time and again. Spontaneous organization of council systems occurred in all revolutions, in the French Revolution, with Jefferson in the American Revolution, in the Parisian commune, in the Russian revolutions, in the wake of the revolutions in Germany and Austria at the end of World War I, finally in the Hungarian Revolution. What is more, they never came into being as a result of a conscious revolutionary tradition or theory, but entirely spontaneously, each time as though there had never been anything of the sort before. Hence the council system seems to correspond to and to spring from the very experience of political action.

In this direction, I think, there must be something to be found, a completely different principle of organization, which begins from below, continues upward, and finally leads to a parliament. But we can't talk about that now. And it is not necessary, since important studies on this subject have been published in recent years in France and Germany, and anyone seriously interested can inform himself.

To prevent a misunderstanding that might easily occur today, I must say that the communes of hippies and dropouts have nothing to do with this. On the contrary, a renunciation of the whole of public life, of politics in general, is at their foundation; they are refuges for people who have suffered political shipwreck—and as such they are completely justified on personal grounds. I find the forms of these communes very often grotesque—in Germany as well as in America—but I understand them and have nothing against them. Politically they are meaningless. The councils desire the exact opposite, even if they begin very small—as neighborhood councils, professional councils, councils within factories, apartment houses, and so on. There are, indeed, councils of the most various kinds, by no means only workers' councils; workers' councils are a special case in this field.

The councils say: We want to participate, we want to debate, we want to make our voices heard in public, and we want to have a possibility to determine the political course of our country. Since the country is too big for all of us to come together and determine our fate, we need a number of public spaces within it. The booth in which we deposit our ballots is unquestionably too small, for this booth has room for only one. The parties are completely unsuitable; there we are, most of us, nothing but the manipulated electorate. But if only ten of us are sitting around a table, each expressing his opinion, each hearing the opinions of others, then a rational formation of opinion can take place through the exchange of opinions. There, too, it will become clear which one of us is best suited to present our view before the next higher council, where in turn our view will be clarified through the influence of other views, revised, or proved wrong.

By no means every resident of a country needs to be a member in such councils. Not everyone wants to or has to concern himself with public affairs. In this fashion a self-selective process is possible that would draw together a true political elite in a country. Anyone who is not interested in public affairs will simply have to be satisfied with their being decided without him. But each person must be given the opportunity.

In this direction I see the possibility 'of forming a new concept of the state. A council-state of this sort, to which the principle of sovereignty would be wholly alien, would be admirably suited to federations of the most various kinds, especially because in it power would be constituted horizontally and not vertically. But if you ask me now what prospect it has of being realized, then I must say to you: Very slight, if at all. And yet perhaps, after all—in the wake of the next revolution.

INDEX

Adams, John, 86n
Adenauer, Konrad, 229
Africa, 209, 210
Agnew, Spiro, 18
Algeria, 152, 194
Alsop, Stewart, 197
American Revolution, 83, 108, 205, 231
Aristotle, 62
Aron, Raymond, 148n, 185, 186
Asia, 25, 26, 40, 209
Association of the Bar of the City of New York, 51, 52n
Auschwitz trial, 71n

Baker v. *Carr*, 100n
Bakunin, Mikhail, 185
Ball, George, 27
Bancroft, George, 91
Barion, Jacob, 114n
Barnes, Peter, 131n
Barnet, Richard J., 4n, 9, 19, 20, 31n, 33n, 37n, 38n, 41n
Barnett, Ross, 64
Bay, Christian, 64n, 82n, 84n
Beaufre, André, 107
Bell, Daniel, 170, 196
Bergson, Henri, 114, 167, 170, 171
Berkeley, 118n, 130, 144n, 153, 187, 190, 202
Berlin, Isaiah, 129n

Bickle, Alexander M., 100n
Bidault, Georges, 194
Black, Charles L., 53n
Bloch, Ernst, 204, 205, 206, 207
Bodin, Jean, 137
Böll, Heinrich, 145
Bonn, 227
Borkenau, Franz, 146n
Brest-Litovsk, 134n
Brzezinski, Zbigniew, 188, 189

Calder, Nigel, 105, 107, 112n, 159n
Calhoun, John C., 76
Cambodia, 24, 75
Camus, Albert, 64
Canossa, 149
Castro, Fidel, 123n
Catherine the Great, 171
Central America, 90
Central Intelligence Agency, 22, 24, 190
Chicago, 153
China, 14, 26, 27, 29, 42, 123n, 221
Chinese revolution, 27, 31
Chomsky, Noam, 109, 116n, 125n, 147n, 161n, 189, 196
Chou En-lai, 29
Cicero, 142n